The Shetland Trader

Book Three: Heritage

Gudrun Johnston

POM POM PRESS
LONDON

Published in 2021 by Pom Pom Press
Text © Gudrun Johnston
Photographs © Ali Denney
Schematic Illustrations © Maya Durham
Botanical Illustrations © Beth Armstrong
Black & White Photographs © Brian Blow

All rights reserved. No portion of this book may be reproduced or transmitted in any form or by any means, mechanical, electronically, photocopying, recording, or otherwise, without written permission of the publisher. For personal use only.

ISBN: 978-1-9160295-7-6
A catalogue record for this book is available from the British Library.

Editors:
Lydia Gluck and Meghan Fernandes

Managing Editor:
Amy Collins

Design:
Bless Design

Publisher and Marketing Director:
Belinda Johnson

UK Wholesale Manager and Community Liaison:
Sophie Heathscott

Features Editor:
Francesca Baldry

Production Coordinator and Retail Manager:
Alice Sleight

Social Media and Digital Content Coordinator:
Sofia Aatkar

Studio Managers:
Anoushka Haroutounian and Gayle Taliaferro Gilner

Copy Editor:
Annie Prime

Consultant:
Emi Ito

Technical Editor:
Jen Arnall-Culliford

Models:
Chelsea Algarin and Heather Krauss

Hair and Makeup:
Mandy Egan

Stylist:
Tessa Dee Miller

Location:
The Hytch at Sierra Water Gardens

Sample Knitters:
Chaitanya Muralidhara, Ellis Greer, Erica Sufka, Irina Lapko, Jessica Rex, Jessica Schwab, Nancy Hunter, Nessy Tania, Nicola Nicholson, Nicole Dupuis, Tammy Sutherland

Yarn Support:
Jamieson & Smith,
Jamieson's of Shetland

Test Knitters:
Allyssa Guzman, Amy Foreman, An-Sofie Alderweireldt, Brunhilde Schober, Cecilia Wranell, Chloe Milward, Christine Wilkerson, Claudia B. Manley, Claudia Siederer, Crystal Hiatt, Dana Hansen, Fiona Donovan, Frauke Urban, Gayle Gansch, Hannah Baker Wester, Jamie Hess, Jennifer Evans, Jeraldine Orlina, Jessica Sherman, Johanne Groulx, Jonna Hartzell, Joy Burkart, Julia Bennett, Juliana Lustenader, Kaitlyn Schauer, Kate Lindstrom, Laura Stanford, Leanne Taylor, Lisa R Wilcox, Maria Dooley, Nicole Fields, Peg Mayor, Rebecca Ranta, Reiko Tashima, Renate Göschel, Rysia Marshall, Sara Greer, Sarah Lindsey, Shawna Jordan, Sigríður Þorsteinsdóttir, Tamara Gonzalez, Valerie O'Keefe, Veena Mosur

Printed in the UK by:
Pureprint Group Limited

For pattern corrections, please visit
pompommag.com/errata

POM POM PRESS
Hackney Downs Studios
Charcoal Hall
Amhurst Terrace
London E8 2BT
United Kingdom
pompommag.com

For Patricia

Contents

10   Editors' Foreword
12   Dad's Foreword

14   Introduction
16   Patricia's Backstory
18   Process

Patterns:
24   - Vair
38   - Maywick
50   - Bunaberry
62   - Willapund
72   - Soorik
86   - Elsk
96   - Hjarta
106   - Vatna
112   - Smora
122   - Snaraness
128   - Tarra

138   Special Techniques
144   Yarn Support
145   Abbreviations
146   Acknowledgements

Editors' Foreword

Gudrun Johnston's work has been a constant presence and inspiration throughout our journeys as knitters and publishers. In our early days as yarn shop assistants, we admired Gudrun's unique vantage point as a modern maker and textile history enthusiast via her self-published *Shetland Trader* series and other patterns. The traditional and venerable Shetland hap shawl was introduced to us and many contemporary knitters by Gudrun herself. Lydia knit the Hansel Hap back in those days, in colours that reminded her of the sea and felt intrinsically connected to the hap's Shetland origins. This shawl was lovingly gifted to a close friend many years later, and continues to keep her warm.

As you will read in the following pages, Gudrun's mother, Patricia Johnston, had also helped popularise Shetland design and tradition decades earlier, through her renowned ready-to-wear knitwear business, also called The Shetland Trader.

Both women have played significant roles in ensuring that Shetland knitting traditions continue to hold a special place in knitters' hearts. The island's methods are revered today among the most distinctive fibre traditions in the world and Shetland is rightfully recognised as the innovative source of numerous techniques we now take for granted and use in myriad ways.

Our own personal interest in fibre art as a form of visual storytelling and cultural record is exemplified in this collection of patterns and writing inspired by Gudrun's mother and Gudrun's experience as a Shetland knitter herself. We view this book as a 21st-century stepping stone in what we know will continue to be a rich knitting heritage, not only for Shetlanders, but all those who love and appreciate Shetland tradition as part of our collective knitting heritage.

Meghan Fernandes & Lydia Gluck
Austin & London
2021

Dad's Foreword

It is a special privilege for me to write the foreword for this book, which contains designs by my daughter Gudrun, based on and inspired by the knitwear created by her mother Patricia under the banner of The Shetland Trader nearly 50 years ago.

Patricia had an eye for design in art, craft, and utility, and an instinctive understanding of colour. This always showed in how she dressed herself and decorated our many family homes. But it wasn't until she settled in Shetland in 1968 that she found a more creative outlet for these talents - not that she would have presumed to have 'talent'.

At our first Shetland home we had a neighbour called Lizzie Laurenson who was a knitter, like so many women of her generation. Patricia asked her to knit Fair Isle sweaters for our children. Inspired by the beauty and intricacy of what Lizzie produced, Patricia began suggesting her own colourways and then her own designs, learning from Lizzie what was possible while gradually expanding the potential of the Shetland tradition.

When friends and family saw the results, they wanted Patricia's creations too, and soon she had to employ several part-time knitters to fulfil the demand. She realised that she was now running a business, but what to call it? Standing on the quayside one day in Lerwick we noticed the name of a local cargo boat that served the islands and could think of no better name than The Shetland Trader.

The beginnings of the business' success coincided with the birth of Gudrun and our move to Bousta. There, Patricia ran the business as a mail order operation while also sharing a shop in the lanes of Lerwick with friend and fellow knitwear designer Victoria Gibson.

We left Shetland soon after, bringing our family's involvement with The Shetland Trader to an end - or so we thought. So how extraordinary it is that Gudrun should find, long after she left home, that she shared her mother's talents for design and colour, to which she has added her own unique knitting skills. Very sadly, Patricia left us before she could see The Shetland Trader, refitted, sail once again with Gudrun. I'm so proud of them both.

**Laughton Johnston
Sandness, Shetland
2021**

Introduction

I was born in 1974 in Levenwick, Shetland, around the time my mum, Patricia Johnston, established her knitwear business, The Shetland Trader. Mum first designed knitwear for her own children, and there are many photos of the Johnston brood all clothed head-to-toe in Mum's early creative fashions. Later, she passed them down to me for my own children to wear. It is a testament to the endurance of Shetland wool that I still have them in mostly pristine condition all these decades later!

Growing up, I knew that Mum had run a knitwear business, but I relegated it to some distant past. It wasn't something that I heard much about, even from her. I would occasionally look through a folder she kept in her old postmaster's desk that contained images of some of her unique creations. I'd marvel at what she had done, but it wasn't really until I entered the world of knitwear design myself that I was able to properly appreciate her talents and contributions to Shetland.

Each of my many trips back to Shetland came with its own revelation. I have spoken to people familiar with Mum's knitwear legacy, and discovered more of her original garments by way of local exhibitions and friends who had lovingly kept their pieces for all these years.

On one trip to Shetland during the annual Wool Week event in 2014, I learned via social media that a local woman, Wendy Inkster, had two of Mum's original Shetland Trader sweaters in her possession. Wendy runs a business repurposing old sweaters into keepsake bears, and the caption alongside the photo read: "Too nice to cut up?" Not realising that she had no such intention, I told my dad we needed to jump in the car and visit Wendy's studio! Now!

The two sweaters in question were distinctive designs of Mum's, combining Fair Isle and lace in a style that is both vintage and timeless. I had only ever seen them in photos from the 70s. Though it was the first time I had met Wendy, she realised the sweaters' significance and generously gifted them to me. The heartache over thinking they may have been lost helped me to realise how strongly I felt about these sweaters and that not only did I need to write up a pattern for these heirloom pieces, but I should put a whole collection together! The idea took quite some time to percolate. I had to make sure that I was making a suitable tribute to Mum. This collection is the result of a process several lifetimes long, and one that has strengthened my bonds with Shetland, a place to which I now feel I truly belong.

Sadly, during much of my journey of discovery and reconnection, Mum was living with Alzheimer's. She passed away in 2017. Mum was always a giver, a creator, big-hearted, and generous. She never dreamed that her knitwear would have so much longevity, but it seems apt that my parents named the business after a ship, *The Shetland Trader*. It reflects the reciprocity inherent in knitwear traditions, the passing on and sharing of ideas over time and distance. I hope that by bringing her designs back to life in these pages I am both honouring the heritage passed down from her and the legacy that ties me to Shetland.

Patricia's Backstory

Mum was not a Shetlander. Prior to moving there in the late 60s she didn't have much knowledge of the long history of knitting attached to the islands.

Neither was she a knitter (although she did dabble in crochet), and she never became one. Instead, she commissioned local expert knitters to create knits from her descriptions and choices of colour and motif. This was initially just to clothe my siblings and me, but friends became enamoured of her unique designs and began to request pieces for their families.

At the time, many of the traditional Fair Isle motifs and subtle shadings had taken a backseat to a Scandinavian aesthetic: yoked sweaters and cardigans displaying the familiar larger tree and star motifs, often in brighter colours. There is no evidence of a yoked sweater among Mum's designs; she clearly felt a different inspiration. After seeing some old pieces of knitwear by Tom Henderson in the museum in Lerwick, she was inspired to bring back the use of the classic Fair Isle patterns and colours in her own work.

It was shortly after this that she recreated a jumper with these types of traditional motifs and shadings. The original was an adult garment, but she had hers made up for a child. There are images of my sister wearing it and it's one of several pieces Mum kept and passed on to me. I keep it displayed on a child's jumper board in my living room. She also kept the original photo she had taken of the sweater in the museum and, on the back, in her familiar cursive, she noted the colours, presumably to source the yarn from one of the Shetland yarn companies.

Mum then moved toward designing adult garments. I wish I'd had the foresight to ask her about her process when she was still able to tell me, but I only began my own knitwear designs after she had been diagnosed with Alzheimer's. I know that she was influenced by other designers and the fashion of her time: maxi dresses, balloon sleeves, turtlenecks, smocks, and tunics. Mum carefully balanced these shapes with thoughtful placement of Fair Isle and lace motifs, combining old with new and creating innovative pieces as a result.

In the little shop space that she shared with her good friend and fellow knitwear designer Victoria Gibson - situated on Burn's Lane in Lerwick - she decided the best way to get her goods out to the wider world was by implementing a mail order catalogue system. When she placed an ad in a London newspaper, she was not at all prepared for the flood of enthusiastic responses from the south. My father still remembers their surprise when the postman arrived bearing the first sackful of orders!

The brochures sent out to interested customers displayed the garments, and sometimes close-ups of Fair Isle and lace patterns used, alongside a description of each piece and some general background on Shetland Fair Isle traditions. The earlier brochures show the garments modelled, featuring hand-drawn illustrations by my artistic grandmother. Later brochures use flat lay photos of the garments. Everything was made to individual measurements. The customer was able to request variations such as a polo neck instead of crew neck and to select certain colour palettes (with a fair amount of freedom for the knitter to put it together with their own touch). At times, customers requested something even more personalised. This information was passed along to the knitter and, after about 4-6 weeks, the item was sent directly to the customer. The result was that each piece really was an original creation.

Mum made sure that her pricing reflected the expert work involved in these creations, and that the knitters were extremely well compensated. Considering the impact that the oil industry had on knitting by luring makers to other types of work, it is remarkable that several designers, including Mum, were able to carve out niches with their cottage businesses. Among the other designers setting up at a similar time and going on to make substantial contributions to the maintenance and growth of knitwear traditions in Shetland were Victoria Gibson, Wilma Malcolmson and Margaret Stuart. As Wilma once said to me "every Shetland knitter can really be viewed as a designer in their own right". Given the way in which Mum collaborated with the knitters, I can see this very much being the case. She brought her ideas and tastes to the table but the knitter brought further nuance with their expert skills in blending colours and motifs to create pleasing patterns.

It's incredible to me that Mum accomplished so much during her 4-5 years running the business, especially given the fact that she had four young children at the time. My parents also moved between several homes in Shetland during this period. With one of these dwellings, Little Bousta, Dad took on a huge renovation project, sometimes rowing his boat across from Snaraness to get a few hours of work in on the croft in order to make it habitable before the arrival of my youngest sibling, Jamie! My parents came full circle when they retired to Muckle Bousta, the croft across the bay, many years later. My eldest sibling Sorley is building his home there now too.

Mum's contribution to the knitwear heritage of Shetland was significant. With the help of talented local knitters, her ideas were brought to life and made their way all over the country, with many of those pieces still in existence and treasured by their owners.

The Shetland Trader was a remarkably successful venture and it's a time capsule for a special moment in the history of our family. For a variety of reasons, my parents decided to move away from Shetland in 1979 and sold the business to a woman called Hilary Salmond, who kept it on as a shop in Edinburgh for a brief period of time.

Mum was seldom idle, always up before any of us and completing multiple tasks before we would emerge from our beds. She always threw herself fully and meticulously into any project. She went on to apply her skills to many things over the years, all the while nurturing and providing for her children. We fondly remember her great qualities and, in particular, her innate selflessness, always putting us before herself. She encouraged all our endeavours, picked us up when we fell, and made us feel fully supported and loved.

This book, which owes everything to Mum's artistry and vision, is a thank you to her.

Process

As soon as I received those original Shetland Trader sweaters from Wendy Inkster, I headed straight to the Woolbrokers in Lerwick, workplace of vintage knitwear aficionada Ella Gordon. I knew that not only would she appreciate seeing these beautiful pieces but she could apply her expertise to matching the original colours as closely as possible. Armed with lots of wool (I knew I had a lot of swatching ahead of me), I returned back to the US. However, it would be a while longer before I began the process of recreating this one-of-a-kind design that Mum had so cleverly thought of all those years ago.

It was hard not being able to just call up Mum and ask her questions directly, but I was able to connect with her regardless. I am so grateful that Mum kept a folder of various documents from her time running The Shetland Trader. I have had it in my possession for many years now, and have often looked through the beautiful black and white photos of her designs. But it wasn't until I decided to make this book that I took a closer look at everything. It became a bit like detective work: I had a photo of a design and a description in the brochure, then had to discover how it was actually put together.

It was rewarding to immerse myself in these materials and see her process and inspiration by way of photos with handwritten notes, images taken of knitwear in the museum, and the work of other designers she clearly admired. I even discovered some undeveloped negatives of images we had never seen before. The whole family enjoyed this little window back into 70s Shetland. Of course, during this whole process, I have also had my dad Laughton to help fill in some of the gaps and entertain me with stories of this time.

The first step in planning the book was narrowing down which designs to include. There were so many to choose from! Then I had to figure out whether to focus on replicating the designs exactly, adding my own touch, or creating entirely new designs inspired by her work. Of course, in the end, it was a combination of everything. In the early stages of working on this book, I shared a couple of original pieces on social media and had some great feedback and encouragement that helped with some of my decision making. I knew that the pieces with particularly unique concepts had to be part of the collection. These included the sweaters from Wendy (called Vair in the book), the smock (Soorik), a version of which I had seen on display on Whalsay, the simply adorned balloon sleeve sweater (Bunaberry), and some form of the stunning dresses/skirts that were among Mum's mail order offerings (Elsk and Hjarta). The Razor Shell Lace sweater (Maywick) has been done by many Shetland designers but, as it was one of Mum's favourite pieces, as is clearly seen in photos from that time, I wanted to include my interpretation of it here. She often paired the Razor Shell Lace sweater with a knitted headscarf, so it felt appropriate to add one of those to the collection (Snaraness). Her brochures showed other accessories too, and the two hats included here (Smora Beanie and Beret) are inspired by the type of things she offered.

Some of the shawls that feature in Mum's collections, which were traditional Shetland haps, were worked from the centre out. Traditionally (and more commonly), haps are knit from the outside in, but in certain parts of Shetland they favoured the modern method of working centre out. Mum lived in one of these places (Bigton) when hiring the first knitters for The Shetland Trader and consequently this was the method favoured in her haps.

When I started to knit (and then design) my own haps back in 2009, the modern method quickly became my preference! As many of you probably know, I already have a pattern for a hap so I decided to do a slightly different take on it for this book. The two shawls, Vatna and Tara, are worked from the outside in as one piece. Instead of the traditional Old Shell Lace typically seen in haps, I used the New Shell/Razor Shell Lace pattern which also appears in various iterations in this book.

Patterns weren't written for Mum's designs during the time that she ran the business. The knitters surely kept their own notes about each design, but as it was a mail order affair there was no need to include instructions for the customer.

A big part of my work was figuring out how best to present these designs for a handknitting audience. A lot of the plain (stockinette) knitting would have been done using a knitting machine (with the Fair Isle and lace portions handknit), so I had to do some reverse engineering to see what would make the most sense in terms of construction. The sweaters I got from Wendy were the first ones that I worked on. I wanted to recreate them exactly as they were. When I was ready to begin, I dug out the yarn I had purchased from Jamieson & Smith several years prior and got to work swatching. I was pleasantly surprised to find that my gauge matched the original sweater perfectly! It didn't take me long to knit up an exact replica of the black version of this sweater. I decided to use one of my favourite set-in sleeve constructions, the top-down seamless short-row method, for the balloon sleeves. I have used this on multiple designs over the years but finessed it some more by consulting Elizabeth Doherty's very informative book on this construction, *Top Down: Reimagining Set-in Sleeve Design*.

I love the balloon sleeve look, which has certainly made a comeback recently, but I appreciate it may not be everyone's cup of tea. Just as Mum offered choices to her customers, I have included options for the handknitter. In the case of *Vair*, there is a straight-sleeve version as well as a crew neck alternate to the turtleneck. I also show the lace portion of this sweater worked in a single colour. We ended up with three versions of this sweater to present in the book, so that you can see some of the possibilities. The balloon sleeves show up again in Bunaberry and the two dresses, Elsk and Hjarta. They are all interchangeable, allowing for even more interpretations.

Naturally, all the items were worked in 100% Shetland yarn, as Mum's had been. She used yarn from several different sources in Shetland, and I used Jamieson's (whose mill is down the road from where my dad now lives) and Jamieson & Smith (locally known as The Woolbrokers) wool for the samples in this book. Each garment is shown in both yarns and between the two companies, there are endless colours to pick from. I had a lot of fun swatching!

Beginning with Vair, I slowly and meticulously worked my way through all the other designs, liaising back and forth with my incredible tech editor Jen Arnall-Culliford, whose collaboration and input on this collection has been considerable.

Eventually we were able to enlist sample knitters, then test knitters, which is always an incredibly satisfying stage for a designer.

I had already begun work on this book when I sent an inquiry to Pom Pom about a possible collaboration. I was very pleased at their enthusiastic response and knew they would produce a beautiful book. Disappointingly, the COVID-19 pandemic scuttled our plans for a studio location in London for the photoshoot. I was literally about to board a plane with all the samples when it became clear that travel was to be avoided for now. After a few months of uncertainty and disappointment, I realised I had to make other arrangements. I was rescued by a wonderful soul and friend, Tessa Miller, who runs a local vintage clothing and furniture store here in Reno, Nevada. She has done numerous photoshoots and knew lots of local people to recruit. She brought together the models (Heather Krauss and Chelsea Algarin) and photographer (Ali Denney) in a beautiful botanical location for what turned out to be a very hot summer day! It was wonderful to see the knitwear being worn and admired - despite the heat.

My daughter Maya was originally going to be one of the models but once the schedule was thrown off that wasn't possible. She did, however, draw all the beautiful schematics for the book. As she worked each sketch, she asked when she could have the actual garment, and I seem to have promised several of them to her as a result!

Continuing to keep it in the family, I asked my sister Beth Armstrong to contribute some of her artwork for the book. She came up with some beautiful botanical designs to complement the plant-filled backdrop we used for the photoshoot. Mum was very green-fingered so it felt like another fitting tribute to her to integrate these into the book.

I can't tell you how excited I am to finally deliver this collection to the knitting world. I know it's not the end of this particular journey. With so many of Mum's designs not included here, there is certainly potential for another collection. In the meantime, I can't wait to see your interpretations of the designs in this book.

Vair

Vair: *'great beauty' in Shetland dialect.*

This sweater was the impetus for the whole book. With the unusual combination of lace and Fair Isle plus the signature 70s silhouette in the balloon sleeves and turtleneck, this sweater is truly timeless.

As Mum offered her mail order customers options when ordering knitwear, I thought it would be good to do the same (and balloon sleeves aren't for everyone).

You can choose to mix and match different elements of this sweater, with the choice of crew or turtleneck, balloon or straight sleeves, plain or striped lace.

Three possibilities are given here.

Sizes:
1 (2, 3, 4, 5, 6, 7, 8, 9, 10)
Recommended to be worn with approx 0–2.5cm / 0–1" of negative ease.
See schematic key at the end of the pattern for full details.

Yarn (fingering / 4-ply-weight yarn in the following amounts):

Colourway 1
The model's height is 173cm / 5'8", with a chest circumference of 89cm / 35", and is wearing a size 2 (with striped razor shell body, balloon sleeves and turtle neck) shown in:
Jamieson & Smith 2ply Jumper Weight (fingering / 4-ply-weight; 100% Real Shetland Wool; 115m / 125yds per 25g ball)
MC: Shade 77; 10 (11, 11, 12, 12, 13, 14, 14, 15, 16) balls
CC2: Shade 54; 1 (1, 1, 2, 2, 2, 2, 2, 2, 2) balls
CC4: Shade FC38; 1 (1, 1, 1, 1, 1, 2, 2, 2, 2) balls
and
Jamieson & Smith Shetland Supreme Jumper Weight (fingering / 4-ply-weight; 100% Real Shetland Wool; 172m / 188yds per 50g ball)
CC1: Moorit (2004); 1 ball
CC3: Shaela (2003); 1 (1, 1, 1, 1, 1, 1, 1, 1, 2) balls
OR approx
MC: 1075 (1145, 1215, 1290, 1355, 1430, 1510, 1595, 1680, 1765)m / 1180 (1255, 1330, 1410, 1485, 1565, 1655, 1745, 1840, 1930)yds
CC1: 45 (50, 55, 60, 65, 65, 70, 75, 85, 90)m / 50 (50, 60, 65, 70, 75, 80, 85, 90, 95)yds
CC2: 90 (100, 110, 120, 130, 140, 155, 165, 175, 190)m / 100 (110, 120, 135, 145, 155, 165, 180, 195, 205)yds
CC3: 85 (95, 105, 115, 125, 130, 140, 150, 165, 175)m / 95 (100, 115, 125, 135, 145, 155, 165, 180, 190)yds
CC4: 70 (75, 85, 90, 100, 105, 115, 125, 135, 140)m / 75 (85, 90, 100, 110, 115, 125, 135, 145, 155)yds

Colourway 2
The model's height is 173cm / 5'8", with a chest circumference of 112cm / 44", and is wearing a size 5 (with striped razor shell body, balloon sleeves and crew neck) shown in:
Jamieson's of Shetland Spindrift (fingering / 4-ply-weight; 100% Shetland Wool; 105m / 115yds per 25g ball)
MC: Camel; 9 (10, 11, 11, 12, 13, 13, 14, 15, 15) balls
CC1: Cocoa; 1 ball
CC2: Shaela; 1 (1, 2, 2, 2, 2, 2, 2, 2, 2) balls
CC3: Tundra; 1 (1, 1, 2, 2, 2, 2, 2, 2, 2) balls
CC4: Moorit; 1 (1, 1, 1, 1, 1, 2, 2, 2, 2) balls
OR approx
MC: 950 (1010, 1085, 1150, 1210, 1275, 1345, 1420, 1500, 1580)m / 1040 (1105, 1185, 1260, 1325, 1400, 1475, 1555, 1640, 1730)yds
CC1: 45 (50, 55, 60, 65, 65, 70, 75, 85, 90)m / 50 (50, 60, 65, 70, 75, 80, 85, 90, 95)yds
CC2: 90 (100, 110, 120, 130, 140, 155, 165, 175, 190)m / 100 (110, 120, 135, 145, 155, 165, 180, 195, 205)yds
CC3: 85 (95, 105, 115, 125, 130, 140, 150, 165, 175)m / 95 (100, 115, 125, 135, 145, 155, 165, 180, 190)yds
CC4: 70 (75, 85, 90, 100, 105, 115, 125, 135, 140)m / 75 (85, 90, 100, 110, 115, 125, 135, 145, 155)yds

Colourway 3
The model's height is 173cm / 5'8", with a chest circumference of 89cm / 35", and is wearing a size 2 (with plain MC razor shell body, straight sleeves and turtle neck) shown in:
Jamieson & Smith 2ply Jumper Weight (fingering / 4-ply-weight; 100% Real Shetland Wool; 115m / 125yds per 25g ball)
MC: Shade 4; 11 (12, 13, 14, 15, 16, 17, 18, 19, 20) balls
CC1: Shade 202; 1 ball
CC2: Shade 27; 1 ball
CC3: Shade 3; 1 ball
CC4: Shade 32; 1 ball
OR approx
MC: 1235 (1345, 1455, 1575, 1675, 1785, 1895, 2010, 2165, 2290)m / 1345 (1460, 1585, 1710, 1820, 1940, 2060, 2180, 2350, 2485)yds
CC1: 40 (45, 50, 55, 60, 65, 70, 75, 80, 85)m / 45 (50, 55, 60, 65, 70, 75, 80, 85, 90)yds
CC2: 30 (35, 35, 40, 45, 45, 50, 55, 55, 60)m / 35 (35, 40, 45, 45, 50, 55, 60, 60, 65)yds
CC3: 30 (30, 35, 35, 40, 40, 45, 50, 50, 55)m / 30 (35, 35, 40, 40, 45, 50, 50, 55, 60)yds
CC4: 10 (10, 10, 10, 10, 10, 10, 10, 10, 15)m / 10 (10, 10, 10, 10, 10, 10, 10, 15, 15)yds

Gauge:
27 sts & 32 rounds = 10cm / 4" over Razor Shell Pattern on 3.5mm needles after blocking

27 sts & 34 rounds = 10cm / 4" over Fair Isle Pattern on 3.5mm needles after blocking

27 sts & 40 rounds = 10cm / 4" over St st on 3.25mm needles after blocking

Needles:
3.5mm / US 4 circular needle, 80cm / 32" or 100cm / 40" length (for the body)

3.25mm / US 3 circular needle, 80cm / 32" or 100cm / 40" length (for the body)

3.25mm / US 3 DPNs or long circular needle (if working magic loop for sleeves)

3mm / US 2 DPNs or long circular needle (if working magic loop for sleeves for cuff)

3.25mm / US 3 circular needle, 40cm / 16" length (for neckband)

3.5mm / US 4 circular needle, 40cm / 16" length (for neckband, turtle neck version only)

Always use a needle size that will result in the correct gauge after blocking.

Notions:
4 stitch markers (one of which should be unique for beginning of round), 2 locking stitch markers, waste yarn or stitch holder (for holding live sts), tapestry needle for weaving in ends

Notes:
This sweater is worked in one piece from the bottom up. Front and back are then divided at the underarm and steek stitches are cast on to work the remainder of the upper body in the round. Additional steeks are added for front neck. After the shoulders have been joined stitches are then picked up around the armhole and short rows are worked to shape the sleeve cap. There is a choice of straight or balloon sleeves, as well as crew or turtleneck finishing. It is also possible to switch in the sleeves from Bunaberry or either of the dresses, Elsk and Hjarta.

If extra length is required, add additional rounds of MC Razor Shell Pattern at the start and end of the body.

Stitch Glossary:
Stripe Sequence
Also shown on charts.
Rounds 1–13: MC
Rounds 14–15: CC1
Rounds 16–17: MC
Rounds 18–21: CC1
Rounds 22–23: CC2
Rounds 24–25: CC1 (round 24 is dec)
Rounds 26–29: CC2
Rounds 30–31: CC3
Rounds 32–33: CC2 (round 32 is dec)
Rounds 34–37: CC3
Rounds 38–39: CC4
Rounds 40–43: CC3 (round 40 is dec)
Rounds 44–45: MC
Rounds 46–49: CC3
Rounds 50–51: CC4
Rounds 52–55: CC3 (round 52 is inc)
Rounds 56–57: CC2
Rounds 58–59: CC3
Rounds 60–63: CC2 (round 60 is inc)
Rounds 64–65: CC1
Rounds 66–67: CC2
Rounds 68–71: CC1 (round 68 is inc)
Rounds 72–73: MC
Rounds 74–75: CC1
Rounds 76–89: MC

Razor Shell Pattern (in the round):
Round 1: Purl.
Round 2: [Yo, k3, sk2po, k3, yo, k1] to end.
Rep rounds 1–2 for pattern.

2x2 Rib (in the round):
Round 1: [K2, p2] to end.
Rep round 1 for pattern.

Abbreviations:
ssk (modified): Slip first stitch knitwise, slip next stitch purlwise, knit them together through back loop

wrap and turn: See Special Techniques on page 143.

A full list of abbreviations appears on page 145.

PATTERN BEGINS

BODY
Note: *Instead of breaking yarn for each colour change, splice in the new colour to change at the correct spot (see Special Techniques on page 140).*

Using 3.5mm / US 4 circular needle, 80cm / 32" or 100cm / 40" length, MC and the long-tail method, cast on 216 (236, 256, 276, 296, 316, 336, 356, 376, 396) sts. Join for working in the round being careful not to twist. PM to indicate beg of round.

Round 1: P107 (117, 127, 137, 147, 157, 167, 177, 187, 197), PM, p1, PM, p107 (117, 127, 137, 147, 157, 167, 177, 187, 197), PM, p1. *2 side seam stitches isolated*
Round 2: *K4, [yo, k3, sk2po, k3, yo, k1] 10 (11, 12, 13, 14, 15, 16, 17, 18, 19) times, k3, SM, k1, SM; rep from * once more.
Round 3: P to end, slipping markers.
Last 2 rounds set Razor Shell Pattern.
For plain body version, work as folls using just MC. For stripes, work as written.
Work a further 10 rounds in Razor Shell Pattern using MC.
Work a further 10 rounds in Razor Shell Pattern following the Stripe Sequence from either the chart or written instructions, starting at round 14.

Throughout the following section, keep the Stripe Sequence and Razor Shell Pattern correct by adjusting how many stitches you work at the start and end of the front and back, thus ensuring that the yarn overs and decreases continue to stack correctly.

Shape waist as folls:
Dec round: *K2tog, work patt as set to last 2 sts before marker, ssk, SM, k1, SM; rep from * once more. *4 sts dec; 212 (232, 252, 272, 292, 312, 332, 352, 372, 392) sts rem*
Next round: P to end, slipping markers.

Work 6 rounds in Stripe Sequence and Razor Shell Pattern.

Work dec round once more, then work a purl round. *4 sts dec; 208 (228, 248, 268, 288, 308, 328, 348, 368, 388) sts rem*

Work 6 rounds in Stripe Sequence and Razor Shell Pattern.

Work dec round once more, then work a purl round. *4 sts dec; 204 (224, 244, 264, 284, 304, 324, 344, 364, 384) sts rem*

Work 10 rounds in Stripe Sequence and Razor Shell Pattern.

Shape waist as folls:
Inc round: *Kfb, work patt to 1 st before marker, kfb, SM, k1, SM; rep from * once more. *4 sts inc; 208 (228, 248, 268, 288, 308, 328, 348, 368, 388) sts*
Next round: P to end, slipping markers.

Work 6 rounds in Stripe Sequence and Razor Shell Pattern.

Work inc round once more, then work a purl round. *4 sts inc; 212 (232, 252, 272, 292, 312, 332, 352, 372, 392) sts*

Work 6 rounds in Stripe Sequence and Razor Shell Pattern.

Work inc round once more, then work a purl round. *4 sts inc; 216 (236, 256, 276, 296, 316, 336, 356, 376, 396) sts*

Work 18 rounds in Stripe Sequence and Razor Shell Pattern.

Change to 3.25mm / US 3 circular needle, 80cm / 32" or 100cm / 40" length.
Knit 2 rounds in MC, ending 8 (10, 11, 12, 13, 14, 15, 16, 17, 18) sts before beg of round marker on final round.
Note: *If you would prefer for the Razor Shell body to end at a different point when worn then it is possible to add in more plain rounds of MC at this point.*

Separate Back and Front with steeks
Next round: K next 15 (19, 21, 23, 25, 27, 29, 31, 33, 35) sts (removing markers), then transfer these sts to waste yarn for underarm, k to 7 (9, 10, 11, 12, 13, 14, 15, 16, 17) sts before next side seam marker, k next 15 (19, 21, 23, 25, 27, 29, 31, 33, 35) sts (removing markers) then transfer these 15 (19, 21, 23, 25, 27, 29, 31, 33, 35) sts to waste yarn for underarm, k93 (99, 107, 115, 123, 131, 139, 147, 155, 163) to end of back. *Two sets of 15 (19, 21, 23, 25, 27, 29, 31, 33, 35) underarm sts are set aside; 93 (99, 107, 115, 123, 131, 139, 147, 155, 163) sts rem for each of back and front; 186 (198, 214, 230, 246, 262, 278, 294, 310, 326) sts in total*
Break yarn.

Rejoin yarn to front and work as folls:
Steek cast-on round: K to end of front, PM for start of steek, using the backwards-loop method (see Special Techniques) cast on 9 sts, PM for end of steek, k to end of back, PM for steek, cast on 9 steek sts, PM for beg of round. *186 (198, 214, 230, 246, 262, 278, 294, 310, 326) sts plus 18 steek sts*

Read the following dec round instructions, but do NOT work them. Work armhole dec rounds as described for your size below, using MC throughout.

Double dec round: *K1, sssk, k to 4 sts before steek marker, k3tog, k1, SM, k9, SM; rep from * once more. *8 sts dec*
Single dec round: *K1, ssk, k to 3 sts before steek marker, k2tog, k1, SM, k9, SM; rep from * once more. *4 sts dec*
Plain round: Knit.

Sizes 1 and 2: Work a single dec round, a plain round and then a single dec round. *8 sts dec; 178 (190, –, –, –, –, –, –, –, –) body sts rem; 89 (95, –, –, –, –, –, –, –, –) sts rem for each of front and back, plus 18 steek sts*

Size 3: Work the single dec round three times. *12 sts dec; 202 body sts rem; 101 sts rem for each of front and back, plus 18 steek sts*

Sizes 4–6: Work a double dec round followed by two single dec rounds. *16 sts dec; – (–, –, 214, 230, 246, –, –, –, –) body sts rem; – (–, –, 107, 115, 123, –, –, –, –) sts rem for each of front and back, plus 18 steek sts*

Sizes 7 and 8: Work two double dec rounds followed by a single dec round. *20 sts dec; – (–, –, –, –, –, 258, 274, –, –) body sts rem; – (–, –, –, –, –, 129, 137, –, –) sts for each of front and back, plus 18 steek sts*

Sizes 9 and 10: Work three double dec rounds. *24 sts dec; – (–, –, –, –, –, –, –, 286, 302) body sts rem; – (–, –, –, –, –, –, –, 143, 151) sts for each of front and back, plus 18 steek sts*

Read through the following instructions carefully. At the same time as establishing the colourwork as described below, continue to shape armhole as folls:
Dec 1 st at each armhole edge on every round 0 (0, 2, 4, 5, 7, 7, 7, 8, 11) times, then dec 1 st at armhole edge on every 2nd round 3 (5, 5, 5, 4, 4, 4, 4, 4, 4) times.

Change to 3.5mm / US 4 circular needle, 80cm / 32" or 100cm / 40" length.

Establish colourwork as folls:
Note: *There is 1 selvedge stitch at each end of front and back that is kept in MC. These stitches are included in the following written instructions but do not appear in the charts. Steek stitches are also not included in charts. Steek stitches should alternate between Background Colour (BC) and Pattern Colour (PC) for that row, forming vertical stripes.*

Round 1: *K1 in MC, reading from right to left, work across row 1 of Chart A for your size, starting and ending where indicated for your size and working decs if required, repeating marked section 6 (6, 6, 6, 8, 8, 8, 8, 8, 8) times in total, k1 in MC, SM, k9 steek sts in alternating colours, SM; rep from * once more.

Last round sets Chart A colourwork pattern, edge and steek sts. Continue to work as set, until chart row 24 is complete. *12 (20, 28, 36, 36, 44, 44, 44, 48, 60) sts dec; 166 (170, 174, 178, 194, 202, 214, 230, 238, 242) body sts rem; 83 (85, 87, 89, 97, 101, 107, 115, 119, 121) sts each for front and back, plus 18 steek sts*

Work from Chart B as folls:
Round 1: *K1 in MC, reading from right to left, work across row 1 of Chart B, starting and ending where indicated for your size, repeating marked section 6 (6, 6, 6, 8, 8, 8, 8, 8, 8) times in total, k1 in MC, SM, k9 steek sts, SM; rep from * once more. Keeping pattern lined up as before, work from Chart B with no further shaping, until chart row 26 (26, 30, 32, 33, 35, 1, 3, 6, 9) is complete for the first (first, first, first, first, first, second, second, second, second) time [50 (50, 54, 56, 57, 59, 61, 63, 66, 69) rounds of colourwork in total].

Shape Front Neck
Keep colourwork pattern correct throughout neck and shoulder shaping, and repeat Chart B as required. Work as folls:

Front neck cast-off round: Work 27 (28, 29, 29, 32, 33, 35, 38, 40, 40) sts as set, break CC yarn, cast off centre 29 (29, 29, 31, 33, 35, 37, 39, 39, 41) sts for front neck, rejoin CC yarn, work as set to end. *27 (28, 29, 29, 32, 33, 35, 38, 40, 40) sts rem for both left and right front; 83 (85, 87, 89, 97, 101, 107, 115, 119, 121) sts for back, plus 18 steek sts*

Sizes 1-6 only
Steek cast on and front neck dec round: Work as set to 3 sts before neck cast off, k2tog, k1 with MC, PM for front neck steek, using backward-loop cast on (cast on 1 stitch in MC, 1 st in CC) 4 times, cast on 1 stitch in MC, PM for end of front neck steek, k1 with MC, ssk (modified), work as set to end. *2 sts dec; 9 steek sts added; 26 (27, 28, 28, 31, 32, –, –, –, –) sts for each of left and right front; 135 (139, 143, 145, 159, 165, –, –, –, –) body sts in total, plus 27 steek sts*

Sizes 7-10 only
Steek cast on and front neck dec round: Work as set to 4 sts before neck cast off, k3tog, k1 with MC, PM for front neck steek, using backward-loop cast on (cast on 1 stitch in MC, 1 st in CC) 4 times, cast on 1 stitch in MC, PM for end of front neck steek, k1 with MC, sssk, work as set to end. *4 sts dec; 9 steek sts added; – (–, –, –, –, –, 33, 36, 38, 38) sts for each of left and right front; – (–, –, –, –, –, 173, 187, 195, 197) body sts in total, plus 27 steek sts*

Read the following neck dec round instructions, but do NOT work them. Work neck dec rounds as described for your size below, keeping colourwork pattern correct throughout. Switch to working in just MC if there are insufficient rounds remaining to complete the colourwork motif.
Front neck double dec round: Work as set to 4 sts before neck steek marker, k3tog, k1 in MC, SM, k9 steek sts, SM, k1 in MC, sssk, work as set to armhole steek, SM, k9 steek sts, SM, work across back as set to armhole steek, SM, k9 steek sts. *4 sts dec*
Front neck single dec round: Work as set to 3 sts before neck steek marker, k2tog, k1 in MC, SM, k9 steek sts, SM, k1 in MC, ssk (modified), work as set to armhole steek, SM, k9 steek sts, SM, work across back as set to armhole steek, SM, k9 steek sts. *2 sts dec*

Work front neck double dec round 0 (0, 0, 0, 0, 0, 0, 1, 1, 1) times, then work front neck single dec round 7 (8, 8, 8, 9, 9, 9, 8, 9, 9) times. *14 (16, 16, 16, 18, 18, 18, 20, 22, 22) sts dec; 19 (19, 20, 20, 22, 23, 24, 26, 27, 27) sts for each of left and right front; 121 (123, 127, 129, 141, 147, 155, 167, 173, 175) body sts in total, plus 27 steek sts*

Shape Front Shoulders
Please review Short Rows: Wrap & Turn Method (see Special Techniques) before proceeding.
Work as folls in St st with MC only.
Short row 1 (RS): K to front neck marker, SM, k9, SM, k to 7 (7, 7, 7, 8, 8, 8, 9, 9, 9) stitches before armhole steek marker, wrap and turn.
Short row 2 (WS): P to neck marker, SM, p9, SM, p to 7 (7, 7, 7, 8, 8, 8, 9, 9, 9) stitches before armhole steek marker, wrap and turn.
Short row 3: K to neck marker, SM, k9, SM, k to 6 (6, 7, 7, 7, 8, 8, 9, 9, 9) sts before prev wrapped st, wrap and turn.
Short row 4: P to neck marker, SM, k9, SM, p to 6 (6, 7, 7, 7, 8, 8, 9, 9, 9) sts before prev wrapped st, wrap and turn.
Next row (RS): K to neck marker, SM, k9, SM, k to armhole steek marker, working wraps together with wrapped sts (see Special Techniques), SM, k9, turn (remove marker).
Next row (WS): Cast off 9 armhole steek sts, remove marker, p to neck steek marker, remove marker, cast off 9 neck steek sts, remove marker, p to armhole steek marker, working wraps together with wrapped sts, remove marker, cast off 9 armhole steek sts. Break yarn and fasten off.

Transfer two sets of 19 (19, 20, 20, 22, 23, 24, 26, 27, 27) front shoulder sts to waste yarn.

Shape Back Shoulders
With 3.25mm / US 3 needles of your choice, rejoin MC yarn to 83 (85, 87, 89, 97, 101, 107, 115, 119, 121) back sts.

Short row 1 (RS): K to last 7 (7, 7, 7, 8, 8, 8, 9, 9, 9) sts, wrap and turn.
Short row 2 (WS): P to last 7 (7, 7, 7, 8, 8, 8, 9, 9, 9) sts, wrap and turn.
Short row 3: K to 6 (6, 7, 7, 7, 8, 8, 9, 9, 9) sts before prev wrapped st, wrap and turn.
Short row 4: P to 6 (6, 7, 7, 7, 8, 8, 9, 9, 9) sts before prev wrapped st, wrap and turn.
Next row (RS): K to end, working wraps together with wrapped sts.
Next row (WS): P19 (19, 20, 20, 22, 23, 24, 26, 27, 27), cast off 45 (47, 47, 49, 53, 55, 59, 63, 65, 67) sts, p to end, working wraps together with wrapped sts.

Reinforce and cut open the neck and armhole steeks (see Special Techniques for further instructions).

Join the shoulders with a three-needle cast off as folls:
Turn the knitting to the WS and return the left front and back shoulder sts to needles, with the RS of the fabric facing each other. Using a third 3.25mm / US 3 needle and working from the armhole edge to the neck edge knit together the first stitch from the front needle with the first stitch on the rear needle. *Knit together the next stitch from the front and rear needles. Cast off one stitch on the right needle tip as normal. Rep from * until all stitches have been joined and cast off.

Repeat this process for the right front and back shoulder sts.

SLEEVES (BOTH VERSIONS)
Count 12 (12, 12, 14, 14, 14, 14, 16, 16, 16) rows down from the shoulder seam on each side of the armhole and place a locking marker in the 13th (13th, 13th, 15th, 15th, 15th, 15th, 17th, 17th, 17th) row.

With RS facing, using MC yarn and 3.25mm / US 3 DPNs or long circular needle, and beginning at the shoulder seam, pick up and knit 1 stitch at the shoulder join, PM, pick up and knit 9 (9, 9, 10, 10, 10, 10, 12, 12, 12) sts to marker, pick up and knit 26 (27, 29, 30, 31, 32, 34, 34, 37, 39) sts to bottom of armhole, k7 (9, 10, 11, 12, 13, 14, 15, 16, 17) sts from held underarm sts, PM, k1 centre underarm st, PM, k7 (9, 10, 11, 12, 13, 14, 15, 16, 17) sts along remainder of underarm sts, pick up and knit 26 (27, 29, 30, 31, 32, 34, 34, 37, 39) sts to marker, pick up and knit 9 (9, 9, 10, 10, 10, 10, 12, 12, 12) sts to shoulder seam. PM to indicate beg of round. *86 (92, 98, 104, 108, 112, 118, 124, 132, 138) sts total (2 seam sts with markers either side at top of shoulder and centre underarm)*

Shape Sleeve Cap
Note: Cap is shaped using the Wrap and Turn method of short rows. **Do not** pick up wraps in this section.
Short row 1 (RS): K1 (centre shoulder st), SM, k9 (9, 9, 10, 10, 10, 10, 12, 12, 12), wrap and turn.
Short row 2 (WS): P19 (19, 19, 21, 21, 21, 21, 25, 25, 25) (going past centre shoulder st), wrap and turn.

Short row 3: K to prev wrapped st, knit wrapped st, k1, wrap and turn.
Short row 4: P to prev wrapped st, p wrapped st, p1, wrap and turn.
Short rows 5–6: Rep short rows 3–4 once more.
Short row 7: K to prev wrapped st, knit wrapped st, wrap and turn.
Short row 8: P to prev wrapped st, p wrapped st, wrap and turn.
Rep short rows 7 and 8 a further 14 (14, 16, 17, 18, 19, 21, 21, 24, 26) times, at which point there will be 13 (16, 17, 18, 19, 20, 21, 22, 23, 24) sts rem unworked before the centre underarm marker on each side.

Note: *In the next section you will wrap 2 sts with every turn. Work in the same way as a single wrap and turn but sl 2 sts together instead of 1.*
Short row 1: K to prev wrapped st, knit wrapped st, wrap 2 sts and turn.
Short row 2: P to prev wrapped st, p wrapped st, wrap 2 sts and turn.
Short row 3: K to prev wrapped sts, k2tog, wrap 2 sts and turn. *1 st dec*
Short row 4: P to prev wrapped sts, p2tog, wrap 2 sts and turn. *1 st dec; 84 (90, 96, 102, 106, 110, 116, 122, 130, 136) sts*

Sizes 2-10 only
Short rows 5–6: Rep short rows 3–4 once more. *2 sts dec; – (88, 94, 100, 104, 108, 114, 120, 128, 134) sts*

All sizes
Note: *The final pair of short rows only wraps a single stitch each time.*
Next short row: K to prev wrapped sts, k2tog, wrap 1 st and turn. *1 st dec*
Next short row: P to prev wrapped sts, p2tog, wrap 1 st and turn. *1 st dec; 82 (86, 92, 98, 102, 106, 112, 118, 126, 132) sts*
Next row (RS): K to beg of round marker. Begin working in the round.
Next round: K to prev wrapped stitch, k2tog, k to 1 st before next wrapped st, k2tog, k to end. *2 sts dec; 80 (84, 90, 96, 100, 104, 110, 116, 124, 130) sts rem*

BALLOON SLEEVES
See below for straight sleeve instructions.
Continue to work St st in the round until sleeve measures 14cm / 5½" from underarm *(or for 54 more rounds).*

Inc round: *K1, SM, k2, M1L, k to 2 sts before next marker, M1R, k2, SM; rep from * once more. *4 sts inc*
Knit 7 (7, 8, 8, 9, 9, 10, 12, 16, 20) rounds.
Rep last 8 (8, 9, 9, 10, 10, 11, 13, 17, 21) rounds a further 12 (12, 11, 10, 9, 9, 8, 7, 5, 4) times. *52 (52, 48, 44, 40, 40, 36, 32, 24, 20) sts inc; 132 (136, 138, 140, 140, 144, 146, 148, 148, 150) sts*
Work inc round once more. *4 sts inc; 136 (140, 142, 144, 144, 148, 150, 152, 152, 154) sts*

Knit 4 (4, 0, 9, 8, 8, 9, 4, 6, 3) rounds. If row tension is correct, sleeve now measures 41.5cm / 16½" from underarm.

Dec round: [K2tog] to end, removing all markers except beg of round marker. *68 (70, 71, 72, 72, 74, 75, 76, 76, 77) sts dec; 68 (70, 71, 72, 72, 74, 75, 76, 76, 77) sts rem*
Dec round: K3 (0, 5, 0, 0, 0, 3, 0, 0, 0), [k3 (3, 2, 4, 4, 5, 4, 4, 7, 6), k2tog] to last 5 (0, 6, 0, 0, 4, 6, 4, 4, 5) sts, k to end. *12 (14, 15, 12, 12, 10, 11, 12, 8, 9) sts dec; 56 (56, 56, 60, 60, 64, 64, 64, 68, 68) sts rem*

Change to 3mm / US 2 DPNs or long circular needle.
Work in 2x2 Rib until cuff measures 15cm / 6".
Cast off all sts in rib.

STRAIGHT SLEEVES
Knit 11 (11, 9, 9, 8, 8, 7, 6, 5, 5) rounds.
Dec round: K1, SM, k to 3 sts before underarm marker, k2tog, k1, SM, k1, SM, k1, ssk, k to end. *2 sts dec*
Rep last 12 (12, 10, 10, 9, 9, 8, 7, 6, 6) rounds a further 6 (6, 6, 2, 3, 3, 3, 6, 14, 8) times.
14 (14, 14, 6, 8, 8, 8, 14, 30, 18) sts dec; 66 (70, 76, 90, 92, 96, 102, 102, 94, 112) sts rem

Knit 9 (9, 7, 7, 6, 6, 5, 4, 3, 3) rounds.
Work dec round once more. *2 sts dec*
Rep last 10 (10, 8, 8, 7, 7, 6, 5, 4, 4) rounds a further 4 (4, 7, 12, 13, 13, 16, 16, 10, 19) times. *10 (10, 16, 26, 28, 28, 34, 34, 22, 40) sts dec; 56 (60, 60, 64, 64, 68, 68, 68, 72, 72) sts rem*

Knit 12 rounds. If row tension is correct, sleeve now measures 37cm / 14½" from underarm.

Change to 3mm / US 2 DPNs or long circular needle.
Work in 2x2 Rib until cuff measures 12.5cm / 5", or desired length.
Cast off all sts in rib.

FINISHING
Neckband
Using 3.25mm / US 3 circular needle, 40cm / 16" length, and starting at the right shoulder join, with RS facing, pick up and knit 45 (47, 47, 49, 53, 55, 59, 63, 65, 67) back neck sts, then pick up and knit 13 (14, 14, 14, 15, 15, 16, 17, 18, 18) sts to front neck sts, pick up and knit 29 (29, 29, 31, 33, 35, 37, 39, 39, 41) cast off front neck sts, then pick up and knit 13 (14, 14, 14, 15, 15, 16, 17, 18, 18) sts to left shoulder join. *100 (104, 104, 108, 116, 120, 128, 136, 140, 144) sts*
Join for working in the round and PM for beg of round.

Crew neck
Work in 2x2 Rib for 5 rounds then cast off all sts in rib pattern being careful not to cast off too tightly.

Turtleneck
Work in 2x2 Rib until neckband measures 10cm / 4". Change to 3.5mm / US 4 circular needle, 40cm / 16" length, and continue in 2x2 Rib for another 11.5cm / 4½". Cast off all sts in rib pattern being careful not to cast off too tightly.

Weave in ends. Tack the cut steek edges to the WS of the garment using yarn. Block piece to schematic measurements. See Special Techniques for further information on blocking.

VAIR SCHEMATIC KEY

a. Hip circumference: 81.5 (89, 96.5, 104, 111.5, 119, 126.5, 134, 141.5, 149)cm / 32 (35, 38, 41, 43¾, 46¾, 49¾, 52¾, 55¾, 58¾)"

b. Waist circumference: 77 (84.5, 92, 99.5, 107, 114.5, 122, 129.5, 137, 144.5)cm / 30¼ (33¼, 36¼, 39, 42, 45, 48, 51, 54, 57)"

c. Bust circumference: 81.5 (89, 96.5, 104, 111.5, 119, 126.5, 134, 141.5, 149)cm / 32 (35, 38, 41, 43¾, 46¾, 49¾, 52¾, 55¾, 58¾)"

d. Length to underarm: 28cm / 11"

e. Armhole depth: 19.5 (20, 21, 22, 22.5, 23, 23.5, 24, 25.5, 26.5)cm / 7¾ (8, 8¼, 8½, 8¾, 9, 9¼, 9½, 10, 10¼)"

f. Cross shoulder: 31 (32, 32.5, 33.5, 36.5, 38, 40.5, 43.5, 45, 45.5)cm / 12¼ (12½, 13, 13¼, 14¼, 15, 15¾, 17, 17¾, 18)"

g. Neck drop: 2.5 (3, 3, 3, 3.5, 3.5, 3.5, 3.5, 3.5, 3.5)cm / 1 (1¼, 1¼, 1¼, 1¼, 1¼, 1¼, 1¼, 1½, 1½)"

h. Back neck width: 17 (17.5, 17.5, 18.5, 20, 20.5, 22, 23.5, 24.5, 25)cm / 6¾ (7, 7, 7¼, 7¾, 8¼, 8¾, 9¼, 9¾, 10)"

i. Upper arm circumference: 30 (31.5, 34, 36, 37.5, 39, 41.5, 43.5, 46.5, 49)cm / 11¾ (12½, 13¼, 14¼, 14¾, 15½, 16¼, 17¼, 18¼, 19¼)"

j. Balloon sleeve wrist circumference: 21 (21, 21, 22.5, 22.5, 24, 24, 24, 25.5, 25.5)cm / 8¼ (8¼, 8¼, 9, 9, 9½, 9½, 9½, 10, 10)"

k. Balloon circumference at widest: 51 (52.5, 53.5, 54, 54, 55.5, 56.5, 57, 57, 58)cm / 20¼ (20¾, 21, 21¼, 21¼, 22, 22¼, 22½, 22½, 22¾)"

l. Balloon sleeve length from underarm: 57.5cm / 22½"

m. Straight sleeve wrist circumference: 21 (22.5, 22.5, 24, 24, 25.5, 25.5, 25.5, 27, 27)cm / 8¼ (9, 9, 9½, 9½, 10, 10, 10, 10¾, 10¾)"

n. Straight sleeve length from underarm: 50cm / 19½"

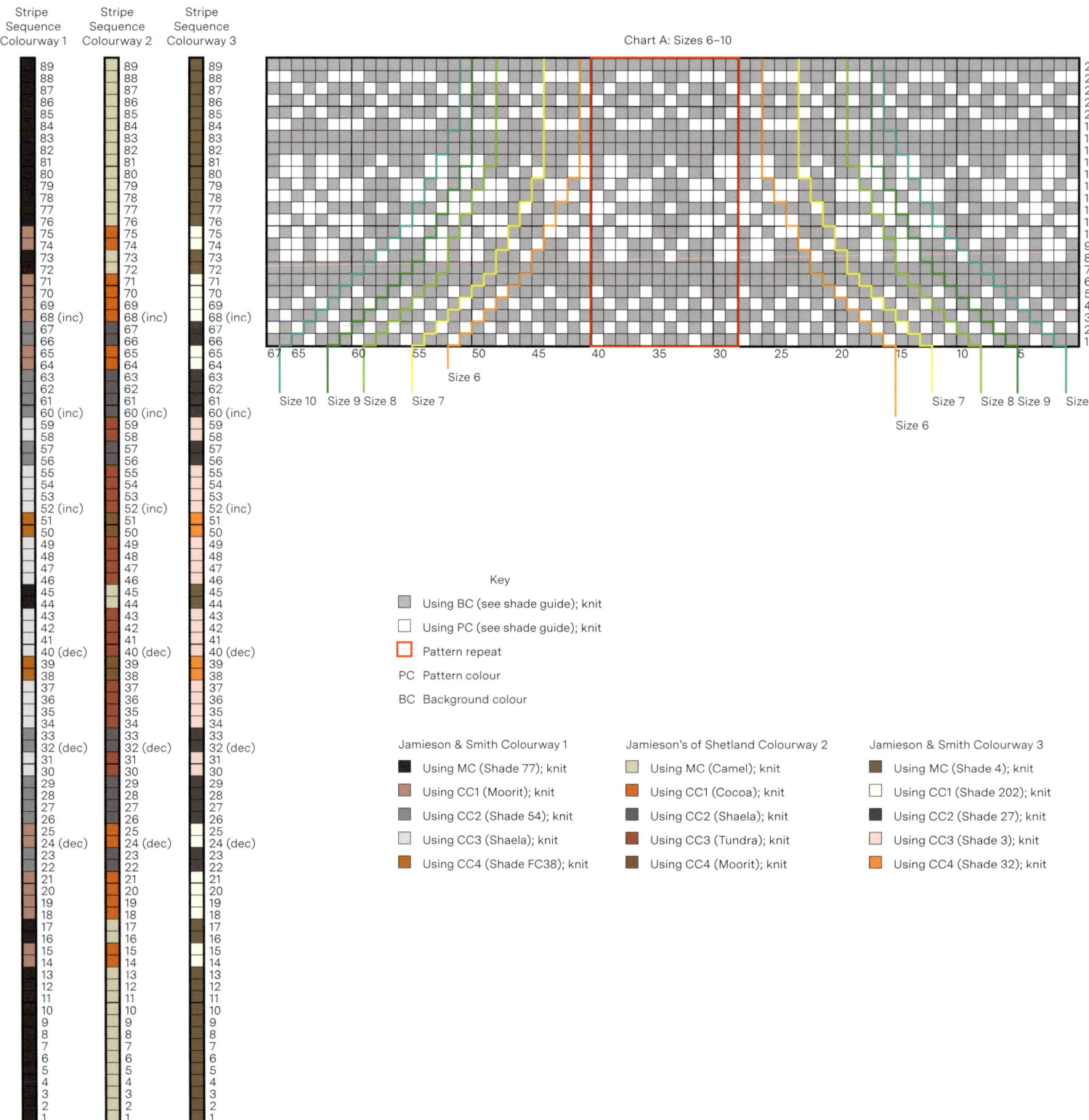

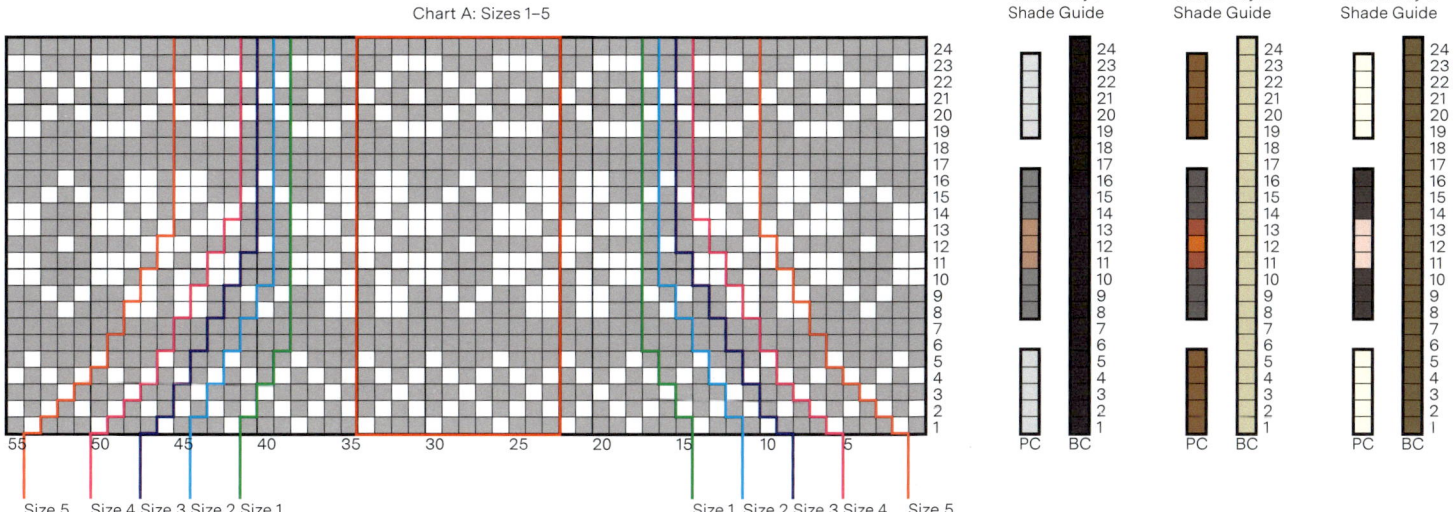
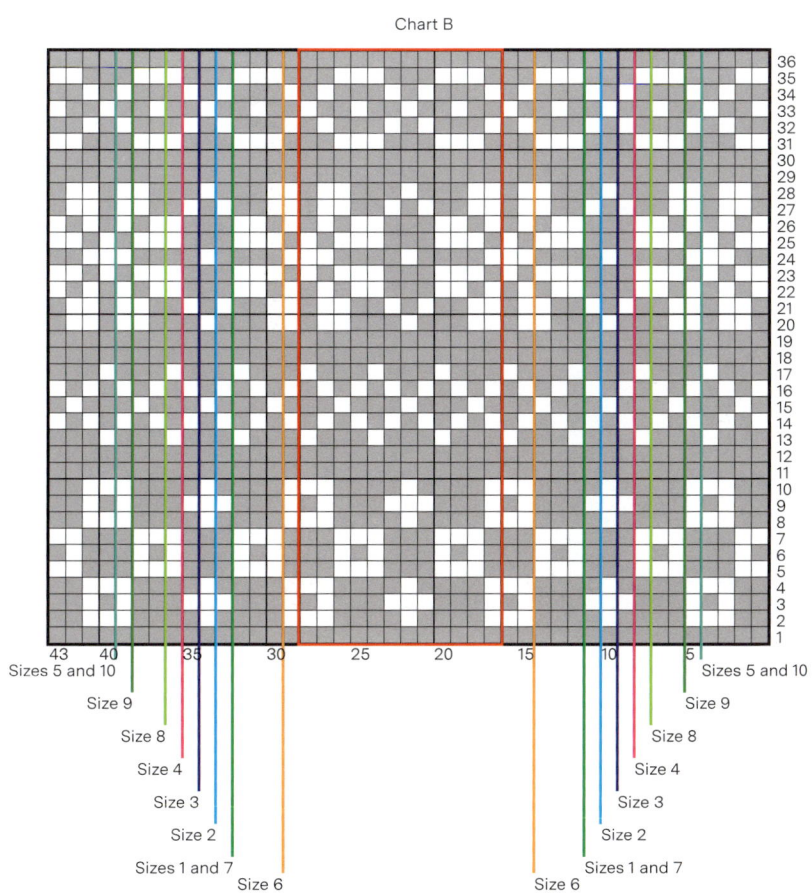
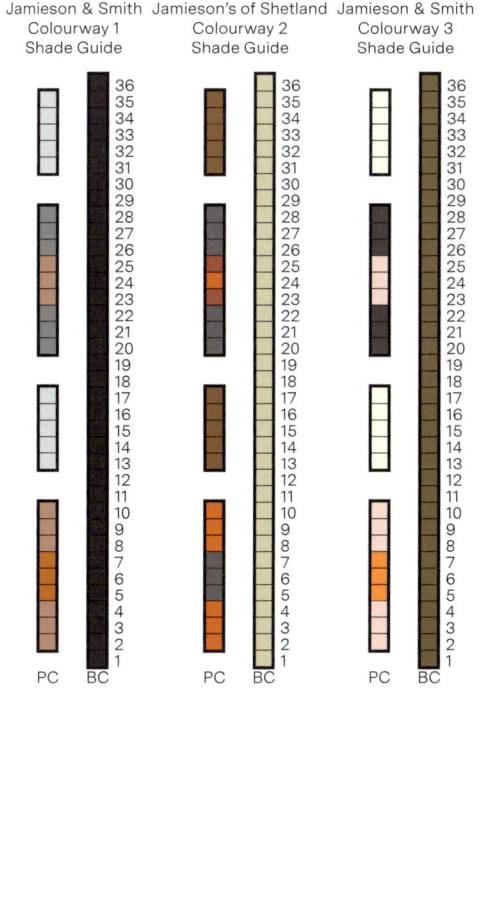

The Shetland Trader / Book Three / Heritage 35

Maywick

Maywick: *the name of the Shetland cottage where my parents spent their honeymoon.*

This all-over Razor Shell Lace sweater was worn frequently by my mother when she ran The Shetland Trader (she is wearing it in the photo on pg 12). Versions of this sweater have been created by many Shetland designers over the years.

I decided to use a simultaneous set-in sleeve construction for this garment, which means there is a lot to keep track of when you work the yoke section.

I am a fan of seamless construction and thought it would work well to keep the Razor Shell Lace following the same direction in the upper body and sleeve area. Razor Shell is a well-known, simple Shetland lace pattern and I use it in multiple designs in this book.

This is definitely best worn with negative ease so that the lace pattern gets stretched open when wearing.

Sizes:
1 (2, 3, 4, 5, 6, 7, 8, 9, 10)
Recommended to be worn with approx 2.5–5cm / 1–2" of negative ease. See schematic key at the end of the pattern for full details.

Yarn (fingering / 4-ply-weight yarn in the following amounts):
MC: 230 (250, 275, 300, 315, 340, 365, 390, 420, 445)m / 250 (275, 295, 325, 345, 365, 395, 425, 455, 485)yds
CC1: 300 (325, 350, 385, 405, 435, 470, 505, 540, 575)m / 325 (350, 380, 420, 440, 475, 510, 550, 585, 625)yds
CC2: 285 (310, 340, 370, 390, 420, 455, 485, 520, 555)m / 310 (340, 370, 400, 425, 455, 490, 525, 565, 600)yds
CC3: 240 (260, 280, 310, 325, 350, 375, 405, 430, 460)m / 260 (280, 305, 335, 355, 380, 410, 440, 470, 500)yds

Colourway 1
The model's height is 173cm / 5'8", with a chest circumference of 89cm / 35", and is wearing a size 1 shown in:
Jamieson's of Shetland Spindrift (fingering / 4-ply-weight; 100% Shetland Wool; 105m / 115yds per 25g ball)
MC: Oxford; 3 (3, 3, 3, 4, 4, 4, 4, 5, 5) balls
CC1: Tundra; 3 (4, 4, 4, 4, 5, 5, 5, 6, 6) balls
CC2: Sholmit; 3 (3, 4, 4, 4, 4, 5, 5, 5, 6) balls
CC3: Yellow Ochre; 3 (3, 3, 3, 4, 4, 4, 4, 5, 5) balls

Colourway 2
The model's height is 173cm / 5'8", with a chest circumference of 112cm / 44", and is wearing a size 5 shown in:
Jamieson & Smith 2ply Jumper Weight (fingering / 4-ply-weight; 100% Real Shetland Wool; 115m / 125yds per 25g ball)
MC: Shade 4; 2 (3, 3, 3, 3, 3, 4, 4, 4, 4) balls
CC1: Shade 32; 3 (3, 4, 4, 4, 4, 5, 5, 5, 5) balls
CC2: Shade 202; 3 (3, 3, 4, 4, 4, 4, 5, 5, 5) balls
CC3: Shade FC61; 3 (3, 3, 3, 3, 4, 4, 4, 4, 4) balls

Gauge:
27 sts & 32 rounds = 10cm / 4" over Razor Shell Pattern on 3.5mm needles after blocking.

Needles:
3.5mm / US 4 circular needle, 80cm / 32" or 100cm / 40" length (for body and yoke)

3.5mm / US 4 DPNs or long circular needle (if working magic loop for sleeves)

3.25mm / US 3 circular needle, 40cm / 16" length (for neckband)

Always use a needle size that will result in the correct gauge after blocking.

Notions:
4 stitch markers (one of which should be unique for beg of round), waste yarn or stitch holder (for holding live sts), tapestry needle for weaving in ends

Notes:
This sweater is worked in one piece from the bottom up. The ¾-length sleeves are joined to the body at the underarm and a simultaneous set-in sleeve construction is used to shape the upper body.

This design requires the knitter to keep the lace pattern correct in each section of the work while working shaping, as well as keeping a stripe sequence correct. The Razor Shell pattern can be worked as a half repeat by only having one of the yarn overs of the repeat and replacing the double decrease at the centre with a single decrease (k2tog/ssk depending which end of the pattern the decrease is worked). If there aren't enough stitches for a half repeat then just work the remaining sts in G st.
If you wish to adjust the sleeve or body lengths you will need to adjust the Stripe Sequence so that they meet on the same row at the yoke.

Stitch Glossary:
Stripe sequence
Also shown on charts.
Rounds 1–3: MC
Rounds 4–5: CC1
Rounds 6–7: MC
Rounds 8–11: CC1
Rounds 12–13: CC2 (round 12 second time through is body inc)
Rounds 14–15: CC1
Rounds 16–19: CC2
Rounds 20–21: CC3
Rounds 22–23: CC2 (round 22 is body dec)
Rounds 24–25: MC
Rounds 26–27: CC3
Rounds 28–29: CC1
Rounds 30–31: CC3
Rounds 32–33: MC (round 32 is body dec)
Rounds 34–35: CC2
Rounds 36–37: CC3
Rounds 38–41: CC2
Rounds 42–43: CC1 (round 42 is body dec)
Rounds 44–45: CC2
Rounds 46–49: CC1
Rounds 50–51: MC
Rounds 52–53: CC3
Rounds 54–55: CC1 (round 54 is body inc)
Rounds 56–57: CC3
Rounds 58–61: MC
Rounds 62–63: CC3
Rounds 64–65: CC1 (round 64 is body inc)
Rounds 66–67: CC3
Rounds 68–69: MC
Rounds 70–73: CC1
Rep rounds 12–73 for pattern.

Razor Shell Pattern (in the round):
Round 1: Purl.
Round 2: [Yo, k3, sk2po, k3, yo, k1] to end.
Rep rounds 1–2 for pattern.

Abbreviations:
ssk (modified): Slip first stitch knitwise, slip next stitch purlwise, knit them together through back loop

wrap and turn: See Special Techniques on page 143.

A full list of abbreviations appears on page 145.

PATTERN BEGINS

BODY
Note: *Instead of breaking yarn for each colour change, splice in the new colour to change at the correct spot (see Special Techniques on page 140).*

Using 3.5mm / US 4 circular needle, 80cm / 32" or 100cm / 40" length, MC and the long-tail method, cast on 216 (236, 256, 276, 296, 316, 336, 356, 376, 396) sts. Join for working in the round being careful not to twist. PM to indicate beg of round.

Round 1: P107 (117, 127, 137, 147, 157, 167, 177, 187, 197), PM, p1, PM, p to last st, PM, p1. *2 side seam sts isolated*

Round 2: *K4, [yo, k3, sk2po, k3, yo, k1] 10 (11, 12, 13, 14, 15, 16, 17, 18, 19) times, k3, SM, k1, SM; rep from * once more.
Round 3: P to end, slipping markers.
Last 2 rounds set Razor Shell Pattern.

Work a further 18 rounds in Razor Shell Pattern following the Stripe Sequence from either the chart or written instructions, starting at round 4.

Throughout the following section, keep the Stripe Sequence and Razor Shell Pattern correct by adjusting how many stitches you work at the start and end of the front and back, thus ensuring that the yarn overs and decreases continue to stack correctly (see notes above for working a half repeat).

Shape waist as folls:
Dec round: *K2tog, work in patt as set to last 2 sts before marker, ssk, SM, k1, SM; rep from * once more. *4 sts dec; 212 (232, 252, 272, 292, 312, 332, 352, 372, 392) sts rem*
Next round: P to end, slipping markers.

Work a further 8 rounds in Stripe Sequence and Razor Shell Pattern.

Work dec round once more, then work a purl round. *4 sts dec; 208 (228, 248, 268, 288, 308, 328, 348, 368, 388) sts rem*
Work a further 8 rounds in Stripe Sequence and Razor Shell Pattern.

Work dec round once more, then work a purl round. *4 sts dec; 204 (224, 244, 264, 284, 304, 324, 344, 364, 384) sts rem*
Work a further 10 rounds in Stripe Sequence and Razor Shell Pattern.

Shape waist as folls:
Inc round: *Kfb, work in patt to marker, kfb, SM, k1, SM; rep from * once more. *4 sts inc; 208 (228, 248, 268, 288, 308, 328, 348, 368, 388) sts*

Next round: P to end, slipping markers.
Work a further 8 rounds in Stripe Sequence and Razor Shell Pattern.

Work inc round once more, then work a purl round. *4 sts inc; 212 (232, 252, 272, 292, 312, 332, 352, 372, 392) sts*
Work a further 8 rounds in Stripe Sequence and Razor Shell Pattern.

Work inc round once more, then work a purl round. *4 sts inc; 216 (236, 256, 276, 296, 316, 336, 356, 376, 396) sts*
Work a further 23 rounds in Stripe Sequence and Razor Shell Pattern.
If round tension is correct, work measures 31cm / 12¼" from cast-on edge.

Divide Back and Front
Round 99: P107 (117, 127, 137, 147, 157, 167, 177, 187, 197), SM, p1, SM, p7 (8, 9, 10, 11, 12, 13, 14, 15, 16), place last 15 (17, 19, 21, 23, 25, 27, 29, 31, 33) sts worked onto waste yarn for underarm, removing markers, p to next marker, SM, p1, place the last 8 (9, 10, 11, 12, 13, 14, 15, 16, 17) sts worked and the next 7 (8, 9, 10, 11, 12, 13, 14, 15, 16) sts from beg of next round, onto waste yarn for underarm, removing markers. *Two sets of 15 (17, 19, 21, 23, 25, 27, 29, 31, 33) underarm sts are set aside; 93 (101, 109, 117, 125, 133, 141, 149, 157, 165) sts rem for each of back and front*

Break yarns and set aside.

SLEEVES (Make 2)
Note: *The sleeve shaping is not marked on the charts and Stripe Sequence since it is worked on different rounds for different sizes.*
Using 3.5mm / US 4 DPNs or long circular needle, MC and the long-tail method, cast on 72 (72, 72, 82, 82, 82, 92, 92, 102, 102) sts. Join for working in the round being careful not to twist. PM to indicate beg of round.
Round 1: P to last st, PM, p1. *Centre underarm st isolated*
Round 2: K1, [yo, k3, sk2po, k3, yo, k1] 7 (7, 7, 8, 8, 8, 9, 9, 10, 10) times, SM, k1.
Round 3: P to end, slipping markers.
Last 2 rounds set Razor Shell Pattern.

Size 1 only
Work 95 rounds in Stripe Sequence (starting on round 4) and Razor Shell Pattern as set, thus ending with a pattern round.
Go to "All Sizes".

Sizes 2-10 only
Following Stripe Sequence (starting on round 4) and Razor Shell pattern, continue in pattern as set for another – (40, 30, 40, 34, 22, 26, 20, 22, 20) rounds, thus ending with a purl round.

Inc round: Kfb, work in pattern to marker, kfb, SM, k1. *2 sts inc*
Starting with a purl round, work a further – (9, 9, 9, 7, 7, 7, 5, 7, 5) rounds in Stripe Sequence and Razor Shell pattern.
Repeat last – (10, 10, 10, 8, 8, 8, 6, 8, 6) rounds a further – (0, 2, 0, 2, 5, 4, 7, 5, 8) times. *– (2, 6, 2, 6, 12, 10, 16, 12, 18) sts inc; – (74, 78, 84, 88, 94, 102, 108, 114, 120) sts*

Work inc round once more. *2 sts inc; – (76, 80, 86, 90, 96, 104, 110, 116, 122) sts*
Work – (44, 34, 44, 36, 24, 28, 26, 24, 20) rounds in Razor Shell and stripe pattern, thus ending with a pattern round. If round tension is correct, sleeve measures 31cm / 12¼" from cast-on edge.

All Sizes
Round 99: P to 7 (8, 9, 10, 11, 12, 13, 14, 15, 16) sts before marker, sl rem 8 (9, 10, 11, 12, 13, 14, 15, 16, 17) sts to waste yarn for underarm (removing side seam markers). Sl first 7 (8, 9, 10, 11, 12, 13, 14, 15, 16) sts of round to same piece of waste yarn. *15 (17, 19, 21, 23, 25, 27, 29, 31, 33) underarm sts on waste yarn; 57 (59, 61, 65, 67, 71, 77, 81, 85, 89) sts rem for sleeve*

YOKE
Throughout the yoke, the Razor Shell Pattern needs to be kept correct in each section (divided by stitch markers), so that the lace pattern continues to line up. If you have insufficient stitches to work a full repeat of the Razor Shell Pattern, a half repeat can be worked as described in the notes section opposite. The Stripe Sequence continues throughout the yoke.

Using 3.5mm / US 4 circular needle, 80cm / 32" or 100cm / 40" length, work as folls:
Yoke union round: Patt across 93 (101, 109, 117, 125, 133, 141, 149, 157, 165) sts of back, PM, patt across 57 (59, 61, 65, 67, 71, 77, 81, 85, 89) sleeve sts, PM, patt across 93 (101, 109, 117, 125, 133, 141, 149, 157, 165) sts of front, PM, patt across 57 (59, 61, 65, 67, 71, 77, 81, 85, 89) second sleeve sts. *300 (320, 340, 364, 384, 408, 436, 460, 484, 508) sts in total*
PM to indicate beg of round.
Next round: Purl.

Sizes 5-10 only
Underarm double dec round: *K1, k3tog, work in patt to 4 sts before marker, sssk, k1, SM, k2tog, work to 2 sts before next marker, ssk (modified), SM; rep from * once more. *12 sts dec; 4 on each front/back and 2 each on sleeves*
Next round: Purl.
Rep the last 2 rounds a further – (–, –, –, 1, 3, 5, 7, 9, 11) times. *– (–, –, –, 24, 48, 72, 96, 120, 144) sts dec; . – (–, –, –, 360, 360, 364, 364, 364, 364) total sts rem; 117 sts each front and back; – (–, –, –, 63, 63, 65, 65, 65, 65) sts each sleeve*

All Sizes
Underarm single dec round: *K1, k2tog, work in patt to 3 sts before marker, ssk (modified), k1, SM, k2tog, work to 2 sts before next marker, ssk (modified); rep from * once more. *8 sts dec*
Next Round: Purl.
Rep the last 2 rounds a further 3 (5, 7, 9, 8, 7, 6, 5, 4, 3) times. *32 (48, 64, 80, 72, 64, 56, 48, 40, 32) sts dec; 268 (272, 276, 284, 288, 296, 308, 316, 324, 332) total sts rem; 85 (89, 93, 97, 99, 101, 103, 105, 107, 109) sts each front and back; 49 (47, 45, 45, 45, 47, 51, 53, 55, 57) sts each sleeve*

Now only decreasing on sleeve sts, work as folls:
Sleeve dec round: *Work in patt as set to marker, SM, k2tog, work to 2 sts before next marker, ssk (modified), SM; rep from * once more. *4 sts dec*

Rep sleeve dec round every 2nd round a further 11 (10, 8, 8, 9, 9, 12, 13, 12, 13) times. *48 (44, 36, 36, 40, 40, 52, 56, 52, 56) sts dec; 220 (228, 240, 248, 248, 256, 256, 260, 272, 276) sts rem; 85 (89, 93, 97, 99, 101, 103, 105, 107, 109) sts each front and back; 25 (25, 27, 27, 25, 27, 25, 25, 29, 29) sleeve sts rem*

Sizes 1-6 only
Then rep sleeve dec round on every 4th round a further 3 (3, 4, 3, 2, 2, –, –, –, –) times. *12 (12, 16, 12, 8, 8, –, –, –, –) sts dec; 208 (216, 224, 236, 240, 248, –, –, –, –) sts rem; 85 (89, 93, 97, 99, 101, –, –, –, –) sts each front and back; 19 (19, 19, 21, 21, 23, –, –, –, –) sleeve sts rem*

All Sizes
Work a purl round.

Top sleeve cast-off round: Work in patt as set across sts of back, remove marker, cast off 19 (19, 19, 21, 21, 23, 25, 25, 29, 29) left sleeve sts, remove marker, work across sts of front in patt as set, remove marker, cast off 19 (19, 19, 21, 21, 23, 25, 25, 29, 29) sleeve sts, remove beg of round marker. Break yarn. *2 sets of 85 (89, 93, 97, 99, 101, 103, 105, 107, 109) sts rem for front and back*

You will now be working back and front separately.

FRONT
With 3.5mm / US 4 circular needle, 80cm / 32" length, rejoin yarn (keeping Stripe Sequence correct) to right armhole edge of front, ready to begin a WS row.

When working back and forth, what were purl rounds are now worked as knit on the WS, with what were the pattern rounds now worked as normal, as RS rows.

Work in patt as set for a further 1 (1, 1, 1, 1, 3, 3, 3, 3) rows, ending with a WS row.

Front neck cast off and neck shaping:
Patt across next 25 (26, 27, 29, 30, 30, 31, 32, 33, 34) sts, k2tog, k1, join new ball of yarn and cast off the next 29 (31, 33, 33, 33, 35, 35, 35, 35, 35) sts, k1, ssk, work in patt to end of front. *Two sets of 27 (28, 29, 31, 32, 32, 33, 34, 35, 36) sts for each front*

You will now be working the left front and right front separately.

RIGHT FRONT
Next row (WS): K to 3 sts before end of right front, k2tog, k1. *1 st dec*
Next row (RS): K1, ssk, patt to end of right front. *1 st dec*
Repeat last two rows a further 2 (2, 2, 3, 3, 3, 3, 3, 4, 4) times, then work the WS dec row a further 0 (0, 1, 1, 1, 1, 1, 1, 0, 0) times. *6 (6, 7, 9, 9, 9, 9, 9, 10, 10) sts dec; 21 (22, 22, 22, 22, 23, 23, 24, 25, 26) sts rem for right front*
Work 1 (1, 0, 0, 0, 0, 0, 0, 1, 1) more row (which will be WS).

Right Front Shoulder Shaping
Please review Short Rows: Wrap & Turn Method (see Special Techniques) before proceeding.
Throughout this section, work all short rows in one colour, and only restart the Stripe Sequence where you left off when you return to working full rows.

Work as folls in G st:
Short row 1 (RS): K to 7 (7, 7, 7, 7, 7, 8, 8, 8, 8) sts before end of row, wrap and turn.
Short row 2 (WS): K to end of row.
Short row 3: K to 7 (7, 7, 7, 8, 8, 8, 8, 8, 9) sts before prev wrapped st, wrap and turn.
Short row 4: K to end of row.
Next row (RS): K to end without picking up wraps.
Next row (WS): K to end.
Place sts of right front onto waste yarn or holder.

LEFT FRONT
Work as folls in G st:
Next row (RS): Knit.
Short row 1 (WS): K to 7 (7, 7, 7, 7, 7, 8, 8, 8, 8) sts before end of row, wrap and turn.
Short row 2 (RS): K to end of row.
Short row 3: K to 7 (7, 7, 8, 8, 8, 8, 8, 8, 9) sts before prev wrapped st, wrap and turn.
Short row 4: K to end of row.
Next row (WS): K to end without picking up wraps.
Place sts of left front onto waste yarn or holder.

BACK

With 3.5mm / US 4 circular needle, 80cm / 32" length, rejoin yarn to back sts ready to begin a WS row.
Work 7 (7, 7, 7, 7, 9, 9, 11, 11) rows in patt as set ending with a WS row.

Back neck cast-off row (RS): Work in patt as set across 23 (24, 24, 25, 26, 26, 27, 28, 28, 29) sts, join new yarn and cast off 39 (41, 45, 47, 47, 49, 49, 49, 51, 51) back neck sts, work in patt as set to end of back. *Two sets of 23 (24, 24, 25, 26, 26, 27, 28, 28, 29) back shoulder sts*

Left Back Shoulder Shaping and Neck shaping

Work as folls in G st:
Next row (WS): K across sts of left back shoulder.

Sizes 4-10 only
Next row (RS): K1, ssk, k to end. *1 st dec; – (–, –, 24, 25, 25, 26, 27, 27, 28) sts*
Next row: K to end.

All Sizes
Short row 1 (RS): K1, ssk, k to 7 (7, 7, 7, 7, 7, 8, 8, 8, 8) sts before end of row, wrap and turn. *1 st dec; 22 (23, 23, 23, 24, 24, 25, 26, 26, 27) sts*
Short row 2 (WS): K to end.
Short row 3: K1, ssk, k to 7 (7, 7, 7, 8, 8, 8, 8, 8, 9) sts before previously wrapped st, wrap and turn. *1 st dec; 21 (22, 22, 22, 23, 23, 24, 25, 25, 26) sts rem for left back shoulder*
Short row 4: K to end.
Next row (RS): K to end without picking up wraps.
Next row (WS): K to end.
Place sts of left front onto waste yarn or holder.

Right Back Shoulder Shaping and Neck shaping

With 3.5mm / US 4 circular needle, 80cm / 32" length and yarn already attached to right back shoulder sts, work in G st as folls:
Next row (WS): Knit.

Sizes 4-10 only
Next row (RS): K to last 3 sts, k2tog, k1. *1 st dec; – (–, –, 24, 25, 25, 26, 27, 27, 28) sts*
Next row (WS): Knit.

All Sizes
Next row (RS): K to last 3 sts, k2tog, k1. *1 st dec; 22 (23, 23, 23, 24, 24, 25, 26, 26, 27) sts*
Short row 1 (WS): K to 7 (7, 7, 7, 7, 7, 8, 8, 8, 8) sts before end of row, wrap and turn.
Short row 2 (RS): K to last 3 sts, k2tog, k1. *1 st dec; 21 (22, 22, 22, 23, 23, 24, 25, 25, 26) sts rem for right back shoulder*
Short row 3: K to 7 (7, 7, 7, 8, 8, 8, 8, 8, 9) sts before previously wrapped st, wrap and turn.
Short row 4: K to end.
Next row (WS): K to end without picking up wraps.
Place sts of right front onto waste yarn or holder.

Join Shoulders

Join the shoulders with a three-needle cast off as folls:
Turn the knitting to the WS and return the left front and back shoulder sts to needles, with the RS of the fabric facing each other. Using a third 3.5mm / US 4 needle and working from the armhole edge to the neck edge knit together the first stitch from the front needle with the first stitch on the rear needle. *Knit together the next stitch from the front and rear needles. Cast off one stitch on the right needle tip as normal. Rep from * until all stitches have been joined and cast off.

Repeat this process for the right front and back shoulder sts.

FINISHING

Seam tops of sleeve caps into shoulder. Join underarms using Grafting in Garter Stitch (see Special Techniques).

Neckband

Pick up at a ratio of 1:1 on cast-off sts and 1:1 rows on the neck shaping sections. Exact number of sts is not important.
Using 3.25mm / US 3 circular needle, 40cm / 16" length, MC and starting at right shoulder join, pick up and k 55 (55, 59, 65, 65, 67, 67, 67, 69, 69) sts across back neck, then 57 (57, 59, 65, 65, 67, 67, 67, 71, 71) sts across front neck sts. PM to indicate beg of round. *112 (112, 118, 130, 130, 134, 134, 134, 140, 140) sts total*
Round 1: Purl.
Round 2: Knit.
Rep rounds 1 and 2 once more, then work round 1 once more.
Cast off all sts loosely using the Icelandic Cast-Off (see Special Techniques).

Weave in ends. Block garment to schematic measurements. See Special Techniques for more blocking information.

MAYWICK SCHEMATIC KEY

a. Hip circumference: 81.5 (89, 96.5, 104, 111.5, 119, 126.5, 134, 141.5, 149)cm / 32 (35, 38, 41, 43¾, 46¾, 49¾, 52¾, 55¾, 58¾)"

b. Waist circumference: 77 (84.5, 92, 99.5, 107, 114.5, 122, 129.5, 137, 144.5)cm / 30¼ (33¼, 36¼, 39, 42, 45, 48, 51, 54, 57)"

c. Bust circumference: 81.5 (89, 96.5, 104, 111.5, 119, 126.5, 134, 141.5, 149)cm / 32 (35, 38, 41, 43¾, 46¾, 49¾, 52¾, 55¾, 58¾)"

d. Length to underarm: 31cm / 12¼"

e. Cross shoulder: 32 (33.5, 35, 36.5, 37.5, 38, 39, 39.5, 40.5, 41)cm / 12½ (13¼, 13¾, 14¼, 14¾, 15, 15¼, 15½, 15¾, 16¼)"

f. Neck drop: 4 (4, 4, 5, 5, 5, 5, 5, 5.5, 5.5)cm / 1¾ (1¾, 1¾, 2, 2, 2, 2, 2, 2¼, 2¼)"

g. Back neck width: 16 (17, 18.5, 20, 20, 20.5, 20.5, 20.5, 21.5, 21.5)cm / 6¼ (6¾, 7¼, 7¾, 7¾, 8¼, 8¼, 8¼, 8½, 8½)"

h. Upper arm circumference: 27 (28.5, 30, 32.5, 34, 36, 39, 41.5, 43.5, 46)cm / 10¾ (11¼, 11¾, 12¾, 13¼, 14¼, 15½, 16¼, 17¼, 18)"

i. Sleeve circumference at cast-on edge: 27 (27, 27, 31, 31, 31, 34.5, 34.5, 38.5, 38.5)cm / 10¾ (10¾, 10¾, 12¼, 12¼, 12¼, 13¾, 13¾, 15, 15)"

j. Sleeve length from underarm: 31cm / 12¼"

k. Yoke depth at armhole edge: 18.5 (19, 20.5, 21, 21, 21.5, 22, 23.5, 24, 25.5)cm / 7¼ (7½, 8, 8¼, 8¼, 8½, 8¾, 9¼, 9½, 10)"

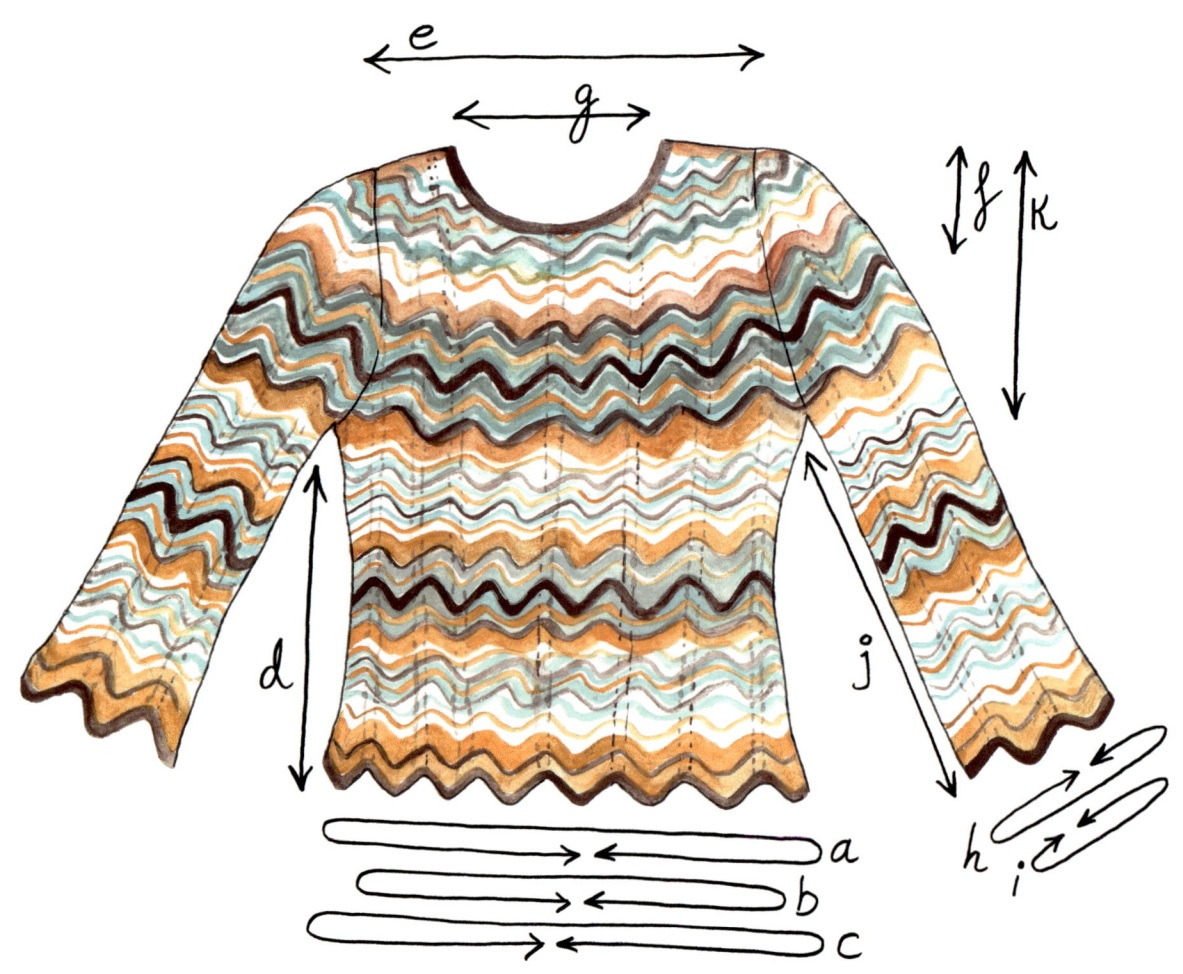

Bunaberry

Bunaberry: *one of the small headlands visible from the croft my dad renovated for us in the 70s (Little Bousta) and my dad's current home (Muckle Bousta).*

After scrutinising one of the old photos from Mum's collection, I realised that what I thought was a dress was actually a turtleneck sweater and vest with a separate long knitted skirt. I then read the description on one of her original brochures that listed these items separately and had an 'aha' moment! However, there was no image of the sweater on its own, so this is my interpretation.

Bunaberry is relatively cropped in length and has the same balloon sleeves as several of the designs in this book. There are two different Fair Isle patterns to choose from to decorate the cuffs, or get creative and insert your own!

The vest pictured over this sweater in the original photo is Willapund on pg 62.

Sizes:
1 (2, 3, 4, 5, 6, 7, 8, 9, 10)
Recommended to be worn with approx 0–2.5cm / 0–1" of negative ease. See schematic key at the end of the pattern for full details.

Yarn (fingering / 4-ply-weight yarn in the following amounts):

Please note, Colourway 1 uses 4 different shades, whereas Colourway 2 uses 6 different shades with a different Fair Isle motif.

Colourway 1
The model's height is 173cm / 5'8", with a chest circumference of 89cm / 35", and is wearing a size 2 shown in:
Jamieson's of Shetland Spindrift (fingering / 4-ply-weight; 100% Shetland Wool; 105m / 115yds per 25g ball)
MC: Moorit; 13 (14, 15, 16, 16, 18, 19, 20, 21, 22) balls
CC1: Camel; 1 ball
CC2: Cocoa; 1 ball
CC3: Auld Gold; 1 ball
OR approx
MC: 1505 (1605, 1710, 1830, 1930, 2115, 2245, 2365, 2500, 2635)m / 1630 (1740, 1860, 1985, 2100, 2300, 2440, 2570, 2720, 2860)yds
CC1: 60 (60, 60, 60, 60, 70, 70, 70, 70, 70)m / 65 (65, 65, 65, 65, 75, 75, 75, 75, 75)yds
CC2: 40 (40, 40, 40, 40, 45, 45, 45, 45, 45)m / 45 (45, 45, 45, 45, 50, 50, 50, 50, 50)yds
CC3: 35 (35, 35, 35, 35, 40, 40, 40, 40, 40)m / 40 (40, 40, 40, 40, 45, 45, 45, 45, 45)yds

Colourway 2
The model's height is 173cm / 5'8", with a chest circumference of 112cm / 44", and is wearing a size 4 shown in:
Jamieson & Smith 2ply Jumper Weight (fingering / 4-ply-weight; 100% Real Shetland Wool; 115m / 125yds per 25g ball)
MC: Shade 32; 12 (13, 14, 15, 16, 17, 19, 19, 21, 22) balls
CC1: Shade 54; 1 ball
CC2: Shade FC61; 1 ball
CC3: Shade FC43; 1 ball
CC4: Shade 125; 1 ball
CC5: Shade FC45; 1 ball

OR approx
MC: 1375 (1465, 1570, 1685, 1780, 1960, 2080, 2185, 2315, 2445)m / 1490 (1590, 1710, 1830, 1935, 2130, 2260, 2375, 2520, 2655)yds
CC1: 70 (70, 70, 70, 70, 80, 80, 80, 80, 80)m / 75 (75, 75, 75, 75, 90, 90, 90, 90, 90)yds
CC2: 55 (55, 55, 55, 55, 65, 65, 65, 65, 65)m / 55 (55, 55, 55, 55, 70, 70, 70, 70, 70)yds
CC3: 20m / 20yds in all sizes
CC4: 20m / 20yds in all sizes
CC5: 20m / 20yds in all sizes

Gauge:
27 sts & 40 rounds = 10cm / 4" over St st on 3.25mm needles after blocking

27 sts & 34 rounds = 10cm / 4" over Fair Isle Pattern on 3.5mm needles after blocking

Needles:
3.25mm / US 3 circular needle, 80cm / 32" or 100cm / 40" length (for body)

3.25mm / US 3 DPNs or long circular needle (if working magic loop for sleeves)

3.5mm / US 4 DPNs or long circular needle (if working magic loop for sleeves)

3mm / US 2 DPNs or long circular needle (if working magic loop for sleeves)

3.25mm / US 3 circular needle, 40cm / 16" length (for neckband)

Always use a needle size that will result in the correct gauge after blocking.

Notions:
4 stitch markers (one of which should be unique for beg of round), 2 locking stitch markers, waste yarn or stitch holder (for holding live sts), tapestry needle for weaving in ends

Notes:
This sweater is worked from the bottom up in the round and then divided at underarm to work front and back separately. The balloon-shaped sleeves are worked top down after picking up stitches around the armhole and the sleeve cap is shaped with short rows. The sleeves have a choice of two Fair Isle bands at the widest point.

Stitch Glossary:
2x2 Rib (in the round):
Round 1: [K2, p2] to end.
Rep round 1 for pattern.

Abbreviations:
wrap and turn: See Special Techniques on page 143.

A full list of abbreviations appears on page 145.

PATTERN BEGINS

BODY
Using 3.25mm / US 3 circular needle, 80cm / 32" or 100cm / 40" length and MC, cast on 216 (240, 264, 288, 312, 336, 360, 384, 408, 432) as folls:
Make a slipknot and place on needle as the first cast-on stitch.
Cast on 1 st using the long-tail method then *cast on 2 sts using the German twisted method (see Special Techniques), then cast on 2 sts using the long-tail method; rep from * until 2 sts rem to cast on, cast on 2 more sts using the German twisted method.
Join for working in the round being careful not to twist. PM to indicate beg of round.

Work in 2x2 Rib until work measures 9cm / 3½" from cast-on edge.
Dec round: *[K2, p2] twice, k2, p2tog; rep from * to end. *18 (20, 22, 24, 26, 28, 30, 32, 34, 36) sts dec; 198 (220, 242, 264, 286, 308, 330, 352, 374, 396) sts rem*
Set-up round: K99 (110, 121, 132, 143, 154, 165, 176, 187, 198) front sts, PM for side seam, k to end.
Work even in St st for 10 rounds.

Inc round: *K2, M1L, k to 2 sts before marker, M1R, k2, SM; rep from * once more. *4 sts inc; 202 (224, 246, 268, 290, 312, 334, 356, 378, 400) sts*
Continue in St st in the round and rep inc round every 12th round a further 4 times. *16 sts inc; 218 (240, 262, 284, 306, 328, 350, 372, 394, 416) sts*
Work even in St st for a further 20 rounds (or until body measures 20.5cm / 8" not including hem), ending 8 (10, 11, 12, 13, 14, 15, 16, 17, 18) sts before beg of the round marker on final round.

Divide Back and Fronts

Next round: K next 16 (20, 22, 24, 26, 28, 30, 32, 34, 36) sts (removing marker), then transfer these sts to waste yarn for underarm, k to 8 (10, 11, 12, 13, 14, 15, 16, 17, 18) sts before next side seam marker, place 93 (100, 109, 118, 127, 136, 145, 154, 163, 172) sts of front just knitted onto waste yarn, k next 16 (20, 22, 24, 26, 28, 30, 32, 34, 36) sts (removing marker), then transfer these 16 (20, 22, 24, 26, 28, 30, 32, 34, 36) sts to waste yarn for underarm, k to end.
Two sets of 16 (20, 22, 24, 26, 28, 30, 32, 34, 36) underarm sts and one set of 93 (100, 109, 118, 127, 136, 145, 154, 163, 172) front sts are set aside; 93 (100, 109, 118, 127, 136, 145, 154, 163, 172) sts rem for back

BACK

Continuing where yarn is attached, work as folls:
**Next row (WS): P93 (100, 109, 118, 127, 136, 145, 154, 163, 172) sts of back.

Read the following dec row instructions, but do NOT work them. Work armhole dec rows as described for your size below, working in St st throughout.
Double dec row: K1, sssk, k to last 4 sts, k3tog, k1. *4 sts dec*
Single dec row: K1, ssk, k to last 3 sts, k2tog, k1. *2 sts dec*

Sizes 1 and 2: Work a single dec row every RS row 5 (7, –, –, –, –, –, –, –, –) times. *10 (14 –, –, –, –, –, –, –, –) sts dec; 83 (86, –, –, –, –, –, –, –, –) back sts rem*

Sizes 3–10: Work a double dec row every RS row – (–, 3, 4, 5, 6, 7, 7, 8, 9) times, then work a single dec row every RS row – (–, 5, 6, 5, 5, 5, 5, 6, 7) times. *– (–, 22, 28, 30, 34, 38, 38, 44, 50) sts dec; – (–, 87, 90, 97, 102, 107, 116, 119, 122) back sts rem*

All Sizes

****Continue in St st for a further 63 (61, 63, 63, 65, 65, 67, 69, 69, 69) rows, beginning and ending with a WS row.

Shape Back Shoulders

Please review Short Rows: Wrap & Turn Method (see Special Techniques) before proceeding.
Short row 1 (RS): K to last 7 (7, 7, 7, 8, 8, 8, 9, 9, 9) sts, wrap and turn.
Short row 2 (WS): P to last 7 (7, 7, 7, 8, 8, 8, 9, 9, 9) sts, wrap and turn.
Short row 3: K to 6 (6, 7, 7, 7, 8, 8, 9, 9, 9) sts before prev wrapped st, wrap and turn.
Short row 4: P to 6 (6, 7, 7, 7, 8, 8, 9, 9, 9) sts before prev wrapped st, wrap and turn.
Next row (RS): K to end, working wraps together with wrapped sts.
Next row (WS): P19 (19, 20, 20, 22, 23, 24, 26, 27, 27), cast off 45 (48, 47, 50, 53, 56, 59, 64, 65, 68) sts, p to end, working wraps together with wrapped sts. Transfer both sets of 19 (19, 20, 20, 22, 23, 24, 26, 27, 27) shoulder sts to separate lengths of waste yarn.

FRONT

With 3.25mm / US 3 circular needle, 80cm / 32", reattach yarn to held sts of front, ready to begin a WS row, and work as for Back from ** to ** (to end of armhole shaping). *83 (86, 87, 90, 97, 102, 107, 116, 119, 122) front sts*

All Sizes

Continue in St st for a further 41 (37, 39, 37, 39, 39, 41, 41, 41, 39) rows, beginning and ending with a WS row.

Shape Front Neck

Front neck cast-off row (RS): K26 (27, 28, 29, 32, 33, 35, 38, 38, 39) sts, join new ball of yarn and cast off centre 31 (32, 31, 32, 33, 36, 37, 40, 43, 44) sts for front neck, k to end. *26 (27, 28, 29, 32, 33, 35, 38, 38, 39) sts rem for both left and right fronts*

Working right and left front separately now.

RIGHT FRONT

Continuing where yarn is attached, purl across one WS row.
Neck dec row (RS): K1, ssk, k to end. *1 st dec; 25 (26, 27, 28, 31, 32, 34, 37, 37, 38) sts rem*
Continue in St st and rep neck dec row every RS row a further 6 (7, 7, 8, 9, 9, 10, 11, 10, 11) times. *6 (7, 7, 8, 9, 9, 10, 11, 10, 11) sts dec; 19 (19, 20, 20, 22, 23, 24, 26, 27, 27) sts rem*

Continue in St st for another 7 (7, 7, 7, 5, 5, 3, 3, 5, 5) rows beginning and ending with a WS row.

Shape Right Front Shoulder

Short row 1 (RS): K to last 7 (7, 7, 7, 8, 8, 8, 9, 9, 9) sts, wrap and turn.
Short row 2 (WS): P to neck edge, turn.
Short row 3: K to 6 (6, 7, 7, 7, 8, 8, 9, 9, 9) sts before prev wrapped st, wrap and turn.
Short row 4: P to neck edge, turn.
Next row (RS): K to end, working wraps together with wrapped sts
Next row (WS): Purl.
Break yarn. Transfer 19 (19, 20, 20, 22, 23, 24, 26, 27, 27) right shoulder sts to waste yarn.

LEFT FRONT

Continuing where yarn is attached, use 3.25mm / US 3 circular needle, 80cm / 32" length to p across one WS row.
Neck dec row (RS): K to last 3 sts of row, k2tog, k1. *1 st dec; 25 (26, 27, 28, 31, 32, 34, 37, 37, 38) sts rem*
Continue in St st and rep neck dec row every RS row a further 6 (7, 7, 8, 9, 9, 10, 11, 10, 11) times. *6 (7, 7, 8, 9, 9, 10, 11, 10, 11) sts dec; 19 (19, 20, 20, 22, 23, 24, 26, 27, 27) sts rem*
Continue in St st for another 8 (8, 8, 8, 6, 6, 4, 4, 6, 6) rows beginning with a WS row and ending with a RS row.

Shape Left Front Shoulder

Short row 1 (WS): P to 7 (7, 7, 7, 8, 8, 8, 9, 9, 9) sts before end of row, wrap and turn.
Short row 2 (RS): K to neck edge, turn.
Short row 3: P to 6 (6, 7, 7, 7, 8, 8, 9, 9, 9) sts before prev wrapped st, wrap and turn.
Short row 4: K to neck edge, turn.
Next row (WS): P to end, working wraps together with wrapped sts.
Break yarn. Transfer 19 (19, 20, 20, 22, 23, 24, 26, 27, 27) left shoulder sts to waste yarn.

Join the shoulders with a three-needle cast off as folls:
Turn the knitting to the WS and return the left front and back shoulder sts to needles, with the RS of the fabric facing each other. Using a third 3.25mm / US 3 needle and working from the armhole edge to the neck edge knit together the first stitch from the front needle with the first stitch on the rear needle. *Knit together the next stitch from the front and rear needles. Cast off one stitch on the right needle tip as normal. Rep from * until all sts have been joined and cast off.

Repeat this process for the right front and back shoulder sts.

SLEEVES
Count 12 (12, 12, 14, 14, 14, 14, 16, 16, 16) rows down from the shoulder seam on each side of the armhole and place a locking marker in the 13th (13th, 13th, 15th, 15th, 15th, 15th, 17th, 17th, 17th) row.

With RS facing, using MC yarn and 3.25mm / US 3 DPNs or long circular needle and beginning at the shoulder seam, pick up and knit 1 stitch at the shoulder join, PM, pick up and knit 9 (9, 9, 10, 10, 10, 10, 12, 12, 12) sts to marker, pick up and knit 26 (27, 29, 30, 31, 32, 34, 34, 37, 39) sts to bottom of armhole, k7 (9, 10, 11, 12, 13, 14, 15, 16, 17) along underarm sts, PM, k2tog (this will be the centre underarm st), PM, k7 (9, 10, 11, 12, 13, 14, 15, 16, 17) sts along remainder of underarm sts, pick up and knit 26 (27, 29, 30, 31, 32, 34, 34, 37, 39) sts to marker, pick up and knit 9 (9, 9, 10, 10, 10, 10, 12, 12, 12) sts to shoulder seam. PM to indicate beg of round. 86 (92, 98, 104, 108, 112, 118, 124, 132, 138) sts total (2 seam sts with markers either side at top of shoulder and centre underarm. Locking markers can now be removed).

Shape Sleeve Cap
Note: *Cap is shaped using the Wrap & Turn method of short rows. Do not pick up wraps for this section.*
Short row 1 (RS): K1 (centre shoulder st), SM, k9 (9, 9, 10, 10, 10, 10, 12, 12, 12), wrap and turn.
Short row 2 (WS): P19 (19, 19, 21, 21, 21, 21, 25, 25, 25) (going past centre shoulder st), wrap and turn.
Short row 3: K to prev wrapped st, k wrapped st, k1, wrap and turn.
Short row 4: P to prev wrapped st, p wrapped st, p1, wrap and turn.
Short rows 5–6: Repeat short rows 3–4 once more.
Short row 7: K to prev wrapped st, k wrapped st, wrap and turn.
Short row 8: P to prev wrapped st, p wrapped st, wrap and turn.
Rep short rows 7 and 8 a further 14 (14, 16, 17, 18, 19, 21, 21, 24, 26) times, at which point there will be 13 (16, 17, 18, 19, 20, 21, 22, 23, 24) sts remaining unworked before the centre underarm marker on each side.

Note: *In the next section you will wrap 2 sts with every turn. Work the same as a single wrap and turn but slip 2 sts together instead of 1.*
Short row 1: K to prev wrapped st, k wrapped st, wrap 2 sts and turn.
Short row 2: P to prev wrapped st, p wrapped st, wrap 2 sts and turn.
Short row 3: K to prev wrapped sts, k2tog, wrap 2 sts and turn. *1 st dec*
Short row 4: P to prev wrapped sts, p2tog, wrap 2 sts and turn. *1 st dec; 84 (90, 96, 102, 106, 110, 116, 122, 130, 136) sts rem*

Sizes 2-10 only
Short rows 5–6: Repeat short rows 3–4 once more. *2 sts dec; – (88, 94, 100, 104, 108, 114, 120, 128, 134) sts rem*

All Sizes
Note: *The final pair of short rows only wraps a single stitch each time.*
Next short row: K to prev wrapped sts, k2tog, wrap 1 st and turn. *1 st dec*
Next short row: P to prev wrapped sts, p2tog, wrap 1 st and turn. *1 st dec; 82 (86, 92, 98, 102, 106, 112, 118, 126, 132) sts rem*
Next row (RS): K to beg of round marker.

Shape sleeve
Begin working in the round.
Next round: K to prev wrapped stitch, k2tog, k to 1 st before next wrapped st, k2tog, k to end. *2 sts dec; 80 (84, 90, 96, 100, 104, 110, 116, 124, 130) sts rem*
The beg of the round is now moved to the underside of the arm. You will essentially swap the placement of the BOR marker and second marker (still keeping two markers total in place):
Partial round: Make sure that the beg of round marker at top of shoulder now becomes the second marker, k40 (42, 45, 48, 50, 52, 55, 58, 62, 65), replace beg of round marker at the underarm.

Continue to work St st in the round until sleeve measures 5 (6.5, 7.5, 10, 12.5, 14, 14, 14, 14, 14)cm / 2 (2½, 3, 4, 5, 5½, 5½, 5½, 5½, 5½)" from underarm.
Inc round: *K1, SM, k2, M1L, k to 2 sts before next marker, M1R, k2, SM; rep from * once more. *4 sts inc*
Knit 9 (9, 10, 12, 13, 5, 5, 8, 11, 16) rounds. Repeat last 10 (10, 11, 13, 14, 6, 6, 9, 12, 17) rounds a further 8 (7, 6, 4, 3, 8, 7, 5, 3, 2) times. *36 (32, 28, 20, 16, 36, 32, 24, 16, 12) sts inc; 116 (116, 118, 116, 116, 140, 142, 140, 140, 142) sts*

Sizes 1, 2, 4, 5, 6, 8 and 9 only
Work inc round once more. *4 sts inc; 120 (120, –, 120, 120, 144, –, 144, 144, –) sts*

Sizes 3, 7 and 10 only
Inc round: K1, SM, k2, M1L, k to next marker, SM; rep from * once more. *2 sts inc; – (–, 120, –, –, –, 144, –, –, 144) sts*

The second marker can now be removed.

Colourway 1
All Sizes
Knit 2 (7, 5, 7, 6, 3, 9, 3, 9, 6) rounds.
Change to 3.5mm / US 4 DPNs or long circular needle and work Fair Isle Chart as folls:
Round 1: Work across 6 sts from row 1 of Chart A 20 (20, 20, 20, 20, 24, 24, 24, 24, 24) times.
Last round sets chart pattern. Continue to work from chart, changing yarns as indicated, until chart row 37 is complete.

Change to 3.25mm / US 3 DPNs or long circular needle.
Knit 8 rounds straight using MC. If row tension is correct, sleeve now measures 41.5cm / 16½" from underarm.

Colourway 2
All Sizes
Knit 0 (5, 3, 5, 4, 1, 7, 1, 7, 4) rounds.
Change to 3.5mm / US 4 DPNs or long circular needle and work Fair Isle Chart as folls:
Round 1: Work across 24 sts from row 1 of Chart B 5 (5, 5, 5, 5, 6, 6, 6, 6, 6) times.
Last round sets chart pattern. Continue to work from chart, changing yarns as indicated, until chart row 41 is complete.

Change to 3.25mm / US 3 DPNs or long circular needle.
Knit 6 rounds straight using MC. If row tension is correct, sleeve now measures 41.5cm / 16½" from underarm.

All Styles
Dec round: [K2tog] to end. *60 (60, 60, 60, 60, 72, 72, 72, 72, 72) sts dec; 60 (60, 60, 60, 60, 72, 72, 72, 72, 72) sts rem*

Sizes 1-3 only
Dec round: *K13, k2tog; rep from * to end. *4 sts dec; 56 sts rem*

Sizes 4 and 5 only
Next round: Knit.

Sizes 6-10 only
Dec round: *K– (–, –, –, –, 7, 7, 7, 16, 16), k2tog; rep from * to end. *– (–, –, –, –, 8, 8, 8, 4, 4) sts dec; – (–, –, –, –, 64, 64, 64, 68, 68) sts rem*

All Sizes
Change to 3mm / US 2 DPNs or long circular needle.
Work in 2x2 Rib until cuff measures 10cm / 4".
Cast off all sts in rib.

FINISHING
Using 3.25mm / US 3 circular needle, 40cm / 16" length and starting at the right shoulder join, with RS facing, pick up and knit 45 (48, 47, 50, 53, 56, 59, 64, 65, 68) back neck sts, then pick up and knit 14 (16, 17, 19, 19, 20, 20, 22, 22, 22) sts to front neck sts, pick up and knit 31 (32, 31, 32, 33, 36, 37, 40, 43, 44) cast-off front neck sts, then pick up and knit 14 (16, 17, 19, 19, 20, 20, 22, 22, 22) sts to left shoulder join. *104 (112, 112, 120, 124, 132, 136, 148, 152, 156) sts*
Join for working in the round. PM to indicate beg of round.

Crew neck
Work in 2x2 Rib for 5 rounds, then cast off all sts in rib pattern being careful not to cast off too tightly.

Turtleneck
Work in 2x2 Rib until neckband measures 10cm / 4". Change to US 4/3.5mm 40cm / 16" circular needle and continue in rib pattern for another 11.5cm / 4½". Cast off all sts in rib pattern being careful not to cast off too tightly.

Weave in ends. Block garment to schematic measurements. See Special Techniques for more blocking information.

BUNABERRY SCHEMATIC KEY

a. Hip circumference: 81.5 (90.5, 99.5, 108.5, 117.5, 126.5, 135.5, 144.5, 153.5, 162.5)cm / 32 (35½, 39, 42¾, 46¼, 49¾, 53¼, 57, 60½, 64)"

b. Waist circumference: 74.5 (83, 91, 99.5, 107.5, 116, 124, 132.5, 140.5, 149)cm / 29¼ (32½, 35¾, 39, 42¼, 45¾, 49, 52¼, 55½, 58¾)"

c. Bust circumference: 82 (90.5, 98.5, 107, 115, 123.5, 131.5, 140, 148.5, 156.5)cm / 32¼ (35½, 38¾, 42, 45¼, 48½, 51¾, 55, 58¼, 61¾)"

d. Length to underarm: 29cm / 11½"

e. Armhole depth: 19 (19.5, 20.5, 21.5, 22, 22.5, 23.5, 24, 25, 26)cm / 7½ (7¾, 8, 8½, 8¾, 9, 9¼, 9½, 10, 10¼)"

f. Cross shoulder: 31 (32.5, 32.5, 34, 36.5, 38.5, 40.5, 43.5, 45, 46)cm / 12¼ (12¾, 13, 13¼, 14¼, 15, 15¾, 17¼, 17¾, 18)"

g. Neck drop (measured at neck edge): 7 (7.5, 7.5, 8, 8, 8, 8, 8.5, 8.5, 9)cm / 2¾ (3, 3, 3, 3, 3, 3, 3¼, 3¼, 3½)"

h. Back neck width: 17 (18, 17.5, 19, 20, 21, 22, 24, 24.5, 25.5)cm / 6¾ (7, 7, 7½, 7¾, 8¼, 8¾, 9½, 9¾, 10)"

i. Upper arm circumference: 30 (31.5, 34, 36, 37.5, 39, 41.5, 43.5, 46.5, 49)cm / 11¾ (12½, 13¼, 14¼, 14¾, 15½, 16¼, 17¼, 18¼, 19¼)"

j. Balloon sleeve wrist circumference: 21 (21, 21, 22.5, 22.5, 24, 24, 24, 25.5, 25.5)cm / 8¼ (8¼, 8¼, 9, 9, 9½, 9½, 9½, 10, 10)"

k. Balloon circumference at widest: 45 (45, 45, 45, 45, 54, 54, 54, 54, 54)cm / 17¾ (17¾, 17¾, 17¾, 17¾, 21¼, 21¼, 21¼, 21¼, 21¼)"

l. Balloon sleeve length from underarm incl. ribbing: 52.5cm / 20¾"

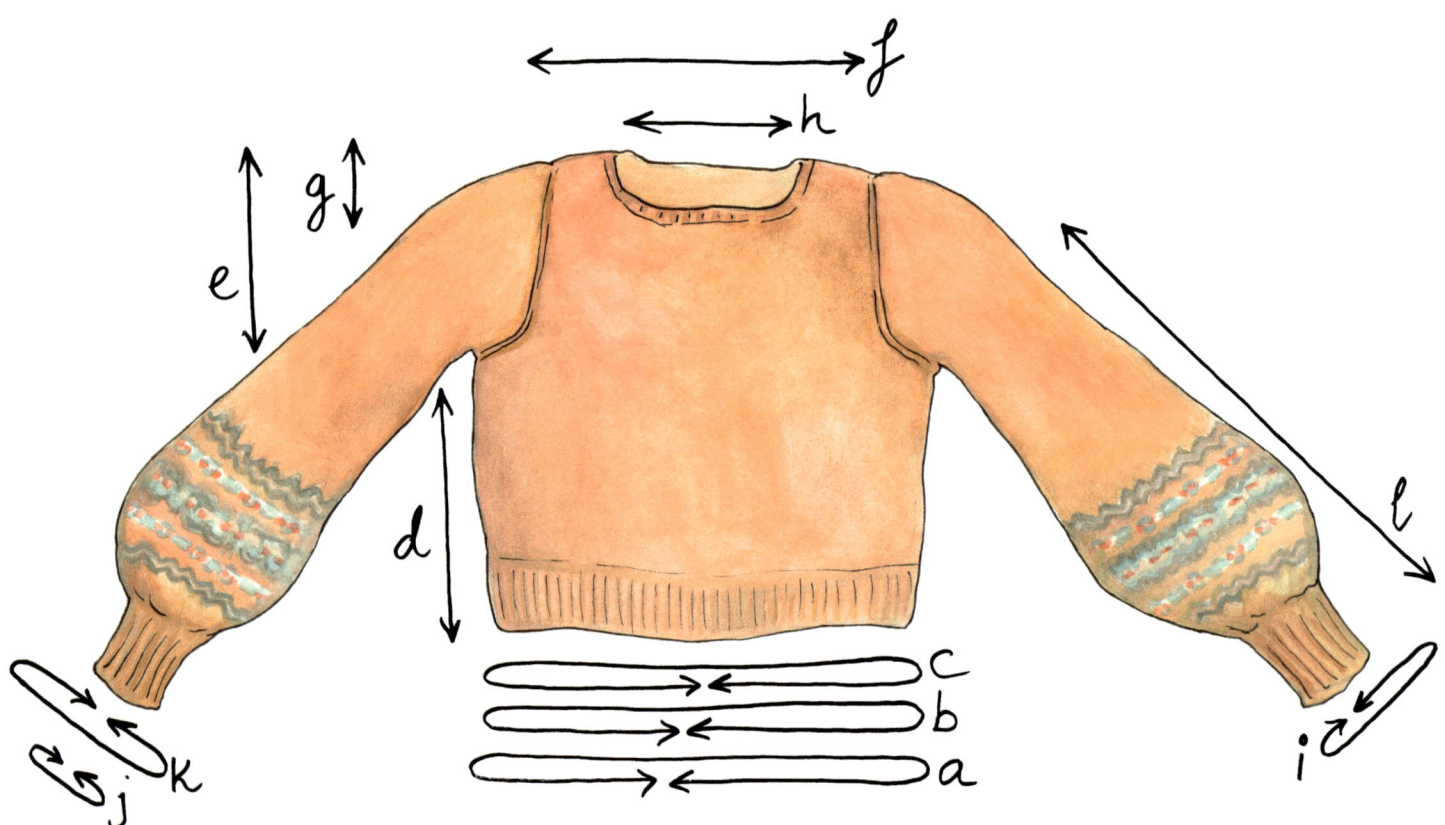

Chart A

Chart B

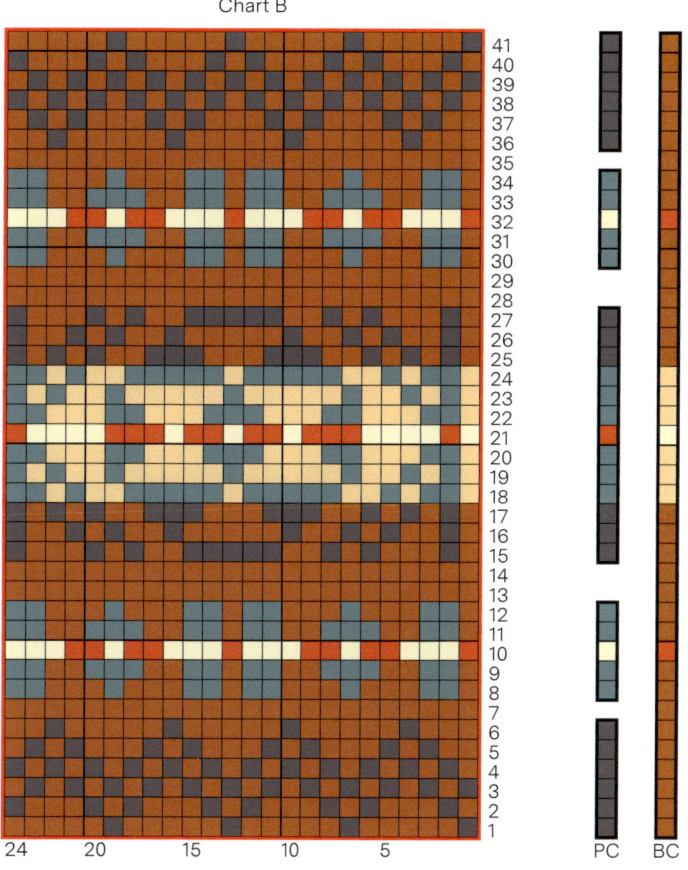

Jamieson's of Shetland
Colourway 1

- Using MC (Moorit); knit
- Using CC1 (Camel); knit
- Using CC2 (Cocoa); knit
- Using CC3 (Auld Gold); knit
- Pattern repeat
- PC Pattern colour
- BC Background colour

Jamieson & Smith
Colourway 2

- Using MC (Shade 32); knit
- Using CC1 (Shade 54); knit
- Using CC2 (Shade FC61); knit
- Using CC3 (Shade FC43); knit
- Using CC4 (Shade 125); knit
- Using CC5 (Shade FC45); knit
- Pattern repeat
- PC Pattern colour
- BC Background colour

The Shetland Trader / Book Three / Heritage

Willapund

Willapund: *a lochan (small loch) on the west side of Shetland, close to our home (Little Bousta) when Mum was running The Shetland Trader.*

This vest is a reinterpretation of one that Mum designed and showed over a balloon-sleeve sweater (see Bunaberry). I chose to go for the same scoop neck style and cropped body but I have used a different motif as the all-over pattern.

If you prefer a longer vest, you can always add length to the hem ribbing or work additional rows of the Fair Isle pattern in the body.

Sizes:
1 (2, 3, 4, 5, 6, 7, 8, 9, 10)
Recommended to be worn with approx 0–2.5cm / 0–1" of positive ease.
See schematic key at the end of the pattern for full details.

Yarn (fingering / 4-ply-weight yarn in the following amounts):

MC: 475 (530, 555, 645, 675, 730, 800, 860, 915, 995)m / 515 (575, 605, 705, 735, 795, 870, 930, 995, 1080)yds
CC1: 160 (180, 190, 220, 230, 250, 270, 290, 310, 335)m / 175 (195, 205, 240, 250, 270, 295, 315, 335, 365)yds
CC2: 120 (135, 140, 164, 170, 185, 200, 215, 230, 250)m / 130 (145, 155, 180, 185, 200, 220, 235, 250, 270)yds
CC3: 140 (155, 160, 190, 195, 215, 235, 250, 265, 290)m / 150 (165, 175, 205, 215, 230, 255, 270, 290, 315)yds

Colourway 1
The model's height is 173cm / 5'8", with a chest circumference of 89cm / 35", and is wearing a size 2 shown in:
Jamieson & Smith 2ply Jumper Weight (fingering / 4-ply-weight; 100% Real Shetland Wool; 115m / 125yds per 25g ball)
MC: Shade 54; 5 (5, 5, 6, 6, 7, 7, 8, 8, 9) balls
CC1: Shade 32; 2 (2, 2, 2, 2, 3, 3, 3, 3, 3) balls
CC2: Shade 3; 2 (2, 2, 2, 2, 2, 2, 2, 2, 3) balls
CC3: Shade 203; 2 (2, 2, 2, 2, 2, 3, 3, 3, 3) balls

Colourway 2
The model's height is 173cm / 5'8", with a chest circumference of 112cm / 44", and is wearing a size 5 shown in:
Jamieson's of Shetland Spindrift (fingering / 4-ply-weight; 100% Shetland Wool; 105m / 115yds per 25g ball)
MC: Moorit; 5 (5, 6, 7, 7, 8, 9, 9, 10) balls
CC1: Camel; 2 (2, 2, 3, 3, 3, 3, 3, 3, 4) balls
CC2: Cocoa; 2 (2, 2, 2, 2, 2, 3, 3, 3) balls
CC3: Auld Gold; 2 (2, 2, 2, 2, 3, 3, 3, 3) balls

Gauge:
27 sts & 34 rounds = 10cm / 4" over Fair Isle Pattern on 3.5mm needles after blocking

28 sts & 44 rounds = 10cm / 4" over 2x2 Rib on 3.25mm needles after blocking

Needles:
3.25mm / US 3 circular needle, 80cm / 32" or 100cm / 40" length (for body)

3.5mm / US 4 circular needle, 80cm / 32" or 100cm / 40" length (for body)

3.25mm / US 3 circular needle, 40cm / 16" length (for arm and neck bands)

Always use a needle size that will result in the correct gauge after blocking.

Notions:
8 stitch markers (one of which should be unique for beg of round), waste yarn or stitch holder (for holding live sts), tapestry needle for weaving in ends

Notes:
This vest is worked in one piece from the bottom up. Front and back are then divided at the underarm and steek stitches are cast on to work the remainder of the upper body in the round. Additional steeks are added for front neck and later, for the back neck. After the shoulders have been joined stitches are then picked up around the armhole and an i-cord cast off is worked to finish the armhole. The neck band is also finished with an i-cord.

Stitch Glossary:
2x2 Rib (in the round):
Round 1: [K2, p2] to end.
Rep round 1 for pattern.

Abbreviations:
ssk (modified): Slip first stitch knitwise, slip next stitch purlwise, knit them together through back loop

A full list of abbreviations appears on page 145.

PATTERN BEGINS

Using CC1 or MC, and 3.25mm / US 3 circular needle, 80cm / 32" or 100cm / 40" length, cast on 216 (240, 252, 276, 288, 312, 336, 360, 384, 396) sts as folls:
Make a slipknot and place on needle as the first cast-on stitch, using the long-tail method, cast on 1 st, *then using the German twisted method (see Special Techniques), cast on 2 sts, then using the long-tail method, cast on 2 sts; rep from * until 2 sts rem to cast on, using the German twisted method, cast on 2 more sts.
Join for working in the round being careful not to twist. PM to indicate beg of round.

Change to MC.
Work in 2x2 Rib for 30 rounds (if row tension is correct, work will measure 7cm / 2¾").
Change to 3.5mm / US 4 circular needle, 80cm / 32" or 100cm / 40" length.

Set-up round: Using MC, k108 (120, 126, 138, 144, 156, 168, 180, 192, 198) sts, PM for side seam, k to end.
Round 1: Work across 6 sts from row 1 of chart 36 (40, 42, 46, 48, 52, 56, 60, 64, 66) times.
Last round sets chart pattern. Continue to work from chart until chart row 7 is complete for the 3rd time (69 rounds of colourwork chart in total).

Divide Back and Fronts
Next round (chart row 8): Remove beg of round marker, k next 6 (8, 9, 10, 11, 12, 13, 14, 15, 16) sts, then transfer these sts to waste yarn for underarm, k to 5 (7, 8, 9, 10, 11, 12, 13, 14, 15) sts before next side seam marker, k next 11 (15, 17, 19, 21, 23, 25, 27, 29, 31) sts (removing marker) then transfer these 11 (15, 17, 19, 21, 23, 25, 27, 29, 31) sts to waste yarn for underarm, k to end, then place last 5 (7, 8, 9, 10, 11, 12, 13, 14, 15) sts worked onto same waste yarn as first 6 (8, 9, 10, 11, 12, 13, 14, 15, 16) sts of round worked. *Two sets of 11 (15, 17, 19, 21, 23, 25, 27, 29, 31) underarm sts are set aside; 97 (105, 109, 119, 123, 133, 143, 153, 163, 167) sts rem for each of back and front; 194 (210, 218, 238, 246, 266, 286, 306, 326, 334) sts in total*
Break yarns, and rejoin to start of front sts.

Steek cast-on round: K1 in MC, work in patt to last st of front, k1 in MC, PM for steek, using the backwards-loop method (see Special Techniques) cast on 9 sts as folls, [cast on 1 st in MC, cast on 1 st in CC] 4 times, cast on 1 st in MC, PM for end of steek, k1 in MC, work in patt to last st of back, k1 in MC, PM for steek, cast on 9 sts as per first steek, PM for beg of round.
194 (210, 218, 238, 246, 266, 286, 306, 326, 334) sts; plus 18 steek sts

Dec round: *K1 in MC, ssk, work patt to 3 sts before steek marker, k2tog, k1 in MC, SM, k9 steek sts, SM; rep from * once more. *4 sts dec; 95 (103, 107, 117, 121, 131, 141, 151, 161, 165) sts rem for each of front and back; 190 (206, 214, 234, 242, 262, 282, 302, 322, 330) sts in total; plus 18 steek sts*

Rep the dec round a further 0 (0, 2, 6, 6, 11, 15, 17, 20, 21) times. *0 (0, 8, 24, 24, 44, 60, 68, 80, 84) sts dec; 95 (103, 103, 105, 109, 109, 111, 117, 121, 123) sts rem for each of front and back; 190 (206, 206, 210, 218, 218, 222, 234, 242, 246) sts in total; plus 18 steek sts*

Rep the dec round every 2nd round a further 7 (10, 9, 7, 7, 5, 3, 2, 2, 2) times. *28 (40, 36, 28, 28, 20, 12, 8, 8, 8) sts dec; 81 (83, 85, 91, 95, 99, 105, 113, 117, 119) sts rem for each of front and back; 162 (166, 170, 182, 190, 198, 210, 226, 234, 238) sts in total; plus 18 steek sts*

Work 7 (1, 1, 8, 8, 7, 8, 8, 5, 14) more rounds in patt as set without decreasing at armhole, thus ending on chart row 31 (31, 31, 7, 7, 7, 8, 8, 8, 18).

Shape Front Neck
Keep colourwork correct throughout neck shaping. Work as folls:

Front neck held sts and steek cast-on round: Work 26 (26, 27, 29, 31, 32, 33, 35, 36, 36) sts as set, sl next 29 (31, 31, 33, 33, 35, 39, 43, 45, 47) sts for front neck to waste yarn, PM for beg of front neck steek, using the backwards-loop method (see Special Techniques) cast on 9 sts [cast on 1 st in MC, cast on 1 st in CC] 4 times, cast on 1 st in MC, PM for end of steek, work as set to end. *26 (26, 27, 29, 31, 32, 33, 35, 36, 36) sts rem each front; 81 (83, 85, 91, 95, 99, 105, 113, 117, 119) sts for back; 133 (135, 139, 149, 157, 163, 171, 183, 189, 191) sts in total; plus 27 steek sts*

Front neck dec round: Work as set to 3 sts before front neck steek marker, k2tog, k1 in MC, SM, k9 steek sts, SM, k1 in MC, ssk (modified), work as set to armhole steek, SM, k9 steek sts, SM, work across back as set to armhole steek, SM, k9 steek sts. *2 sts dec; 25 (25, 26, 28, 30, 31, 32, 34, 35, 35) sts rem for each front*
Repeat the front neck dec round a further 9 (9, 9, 11, 11, 11, 11, 11, 11, 11) times. *18 (18, 18, 22, 22, 22, 22, 22, 22, 22) sts dec; 16 (16, 17, 17, 19, 20, 21, 23, 24, 24) sts rem for each front; 113 (115, 119, 125, 133, 139, 147, 159, 165, 167) sts in total; plus 27 steek sts*

Work a further 27 (27, 27, 29, 29, 29, 31, 31, 31, 31) rounds in patt as set without any shaping, thus ending on chart row 7 (7, 7, 18, 18, 18, 21, 21, 21, 31).

Shape Back Neck
Back neck held sts and steek cast-on round: Work as set to front neck steek marker, SM, k9 steek sts, SM, work as set to armhole steek marker, SM, k9 steek sts, SM, work across 19 (19, 20, 20, 22, 23, 24, 26, 27, 27) sts of back, sl next 43 (45, 45, 51, 51, 53, 57, 61, 63, 65) sts to waste yarn for back neck, PM for beg of back neck steek, using the backwards-loop method (see Special Techniques) cast on 9 sts [cast on 1 st in MC, cast on 1 st in CC] 4 times, cast on 1 st in MC, PM for end of steek, work as set to end of round. *16 (16, 17, 17, 19, 20, 21, 23, 24, 24) sts for each of left and right front; 19 (19, 20, 20, 22, 23, 24, 26, 27, 27) sts for each of left and right back; 70 (70, 74, 74, 82, 86, 90, 98, 102, 102) sts in total; plus 36 steek sts*

Back neck dec round: Work across sts of front as set, SM, k9 armhole steek sts, SM, work to 3 sts before first back neck steek marker, k2tog, k1 in MC, SM, k9 steek sts, SM, k1 in MC, ssk, work as set to end of round. *2 sts dec at back neck; 18 (18, 19, 19, 21, 22, 23, 25, 26, 26) sts for each left and right back*

Work 1 plain round without any shaping. Rep last 2 rounds once more, then work back neck dec round once more. *4 sts dec at back neck; 16 (16, 17, 17, 19, 20, 21, 23, 24, 24) sts for each of left and right front and back; 64 (64, 68, 68, 76, 80, 84, 92, 96, 96) sts in total; plus 36 steek sts*

Next round: *Work as set to steek marker, remove marker, cast off 9 steek sts, remove marker; rep from * a further 3 times. Break yarn and fasten off. Transfer all four sets of 16 (16, 17, 17, 19, 20, 21, 23, 24, 24) shoulder sts to waste yarn.

Reinforce and cut open the neck and armhole steeks (see Special Techniques for further instructions).

Join the shoulders with a three-needle cast off as folls:
Turn the knitting to the WS and return the left front and back shoulder sts to needles. Using a third needle and working from the armhole edge to the neck edge knit together the first stitch from the front needle with the first stitch on the rear needle. *Knit together the next stitch from the front and rear needles. Cast off one stitch on the right needle tip as normal. Repeat from * until all stitches have been joined and cast off.
Repeat this process for the right front and back shoulder sts.

FINISHING
Armhole bands
Using 3.25mm / US 3 circular needle, 40cm / 16" length and MC, starting at underarm held sts, with RS facing, knit across 11 (15, 17, 19, 21, 23, 25, 27, 29, 31) underarm sts, pick up and knit 69 (69, 69, 80, 80, 80, 83, 83, 83, 93) sts up to shoulder, and pick up and knit 69 (69, 69, 80, 80, 80, 83, 83, 83, 93) sts back down to underarm. *149 (153, 155, 179, 181, 183, 191, 193, 195, 217) sts*

Work an i-cord cast off (see Special Techniques) across all sts making sure that the cast off isn't too loose or too tight.

Neckband
Using 3.25mm / US 3 circular needle, 40cm / 16" length and MC, starting at back neck held sts, with RS facing, knit across 43 (45, 45, 51, 51, 53, 57, 61, 63, 65) sts from back neck, pick up and knit 7 sts up back neck shaping to shoulder, pick up and knit 45 (45, 45, 49, 49, 49, 51, 51, 51, 51) sts down to front neck held sts, knit across 29 (31, 31, 33, 33, 35, 39, 43, 45, 47) sts for front neck, pick up and knit 45 (45, 45, 49, 49, 49, 51, 51, 51, 51) sts up to shoulder, and pick up and knit 7 sts down to back neck sts. *176 (180, 180, 196, 196, 200, 212, 220, 224, 228) sts*

Work an i-cord cast off (see Special Techniques) across all sts making sure that cast off isn't too loose or too tight.

Weave in ends. Tack the cut steek edges to the WS of the garment using yarn. Block piece to schematic measurements. See Special Techniques for further information on blocking.

WILLAPUND SCHEMATIC KEY

a. Bust circumference: 81.5 (90.5, 95, 104, 108.5, 117.5, 126.5, 135.5, 144.5, 149)cm / 32 (35½, 37¼, 41, 42¾, 46¼, 49¾, 53¼, 57, 58¾)"

b. Length to underarm: 28cm / 11"

c. Armhole depth: 20.5 (20.5, 20.5, 23.5, 23.5, 23.5, 24.5, 24.5, 24.5, 27.5)cm / 8 (8, 8, 9¼, 9¼, 9¼, 9¾, 9¾, 9¾, 10¾)"

d. Cross shoulder: 30.5 (31, 32, 34, 35.5, 37.5, 39.5, 42.5, 44, 45)cm / 12 (12¼, 12½, 13½, 14, 14¾, 15½, 16¾, 17¼, 17¾)"

e. Back neck width: 18.5 (19, 19, 21.5, 21.5, 22, 23.5, 25, 26, 26.5)cm / 7¼ (7½, 7½, 8½, 8½, 8¾, 9¼, 10, 10¼, 10½)"

f. Neck drop: 13.5 (13.5, 13.5, 14.5, 14.5, 14.5, 15, 15, 15, 15)cm / 5¼ (5¼, 5¼, 5¾, 5¾, 5¾, 6, 6, 6, 6)"

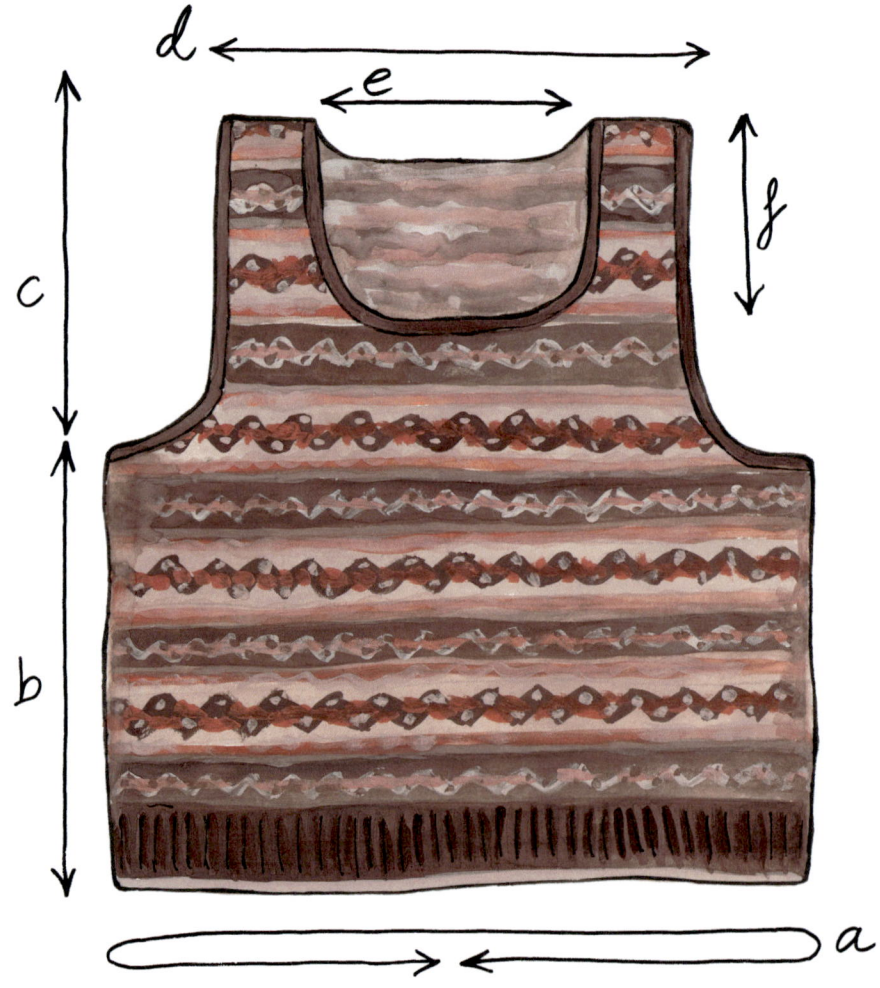

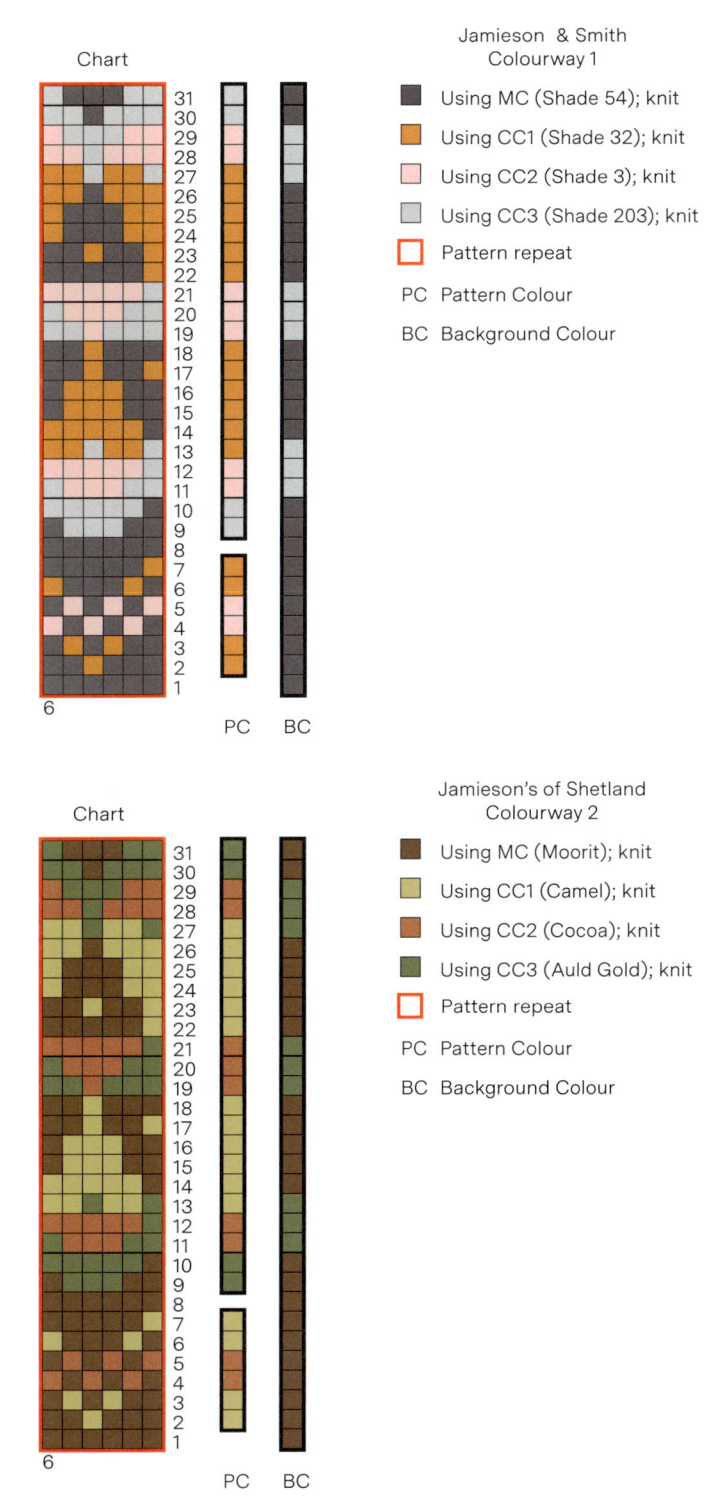

Chart

Jamieson & Smith
Colourway 1

- Using MC (Shade 54); knit
- Using CC1 (Shade 32); knit
- Using CC2 (Shade 3); knit
- Using CC3 (Shade 203); knit
- Pattern repeat

PC Pattern Colour

BC Background Colour

Chart

Jamieson's of Shetland
Colourway 2

- Using MC (Moorit); knit
- Using CC1 (Camel); knit
- Using CC2 (Cocoa); knit
- Using CC3 (Auld Gold); knit
- Pattern repeat

PC Pattern Colour

BC Background Colour

The Shetland Trader / Book Three / Heritage   69

Soorik

Soorik: *'sorrel' in Shetland dialect.*

This smock is another of Mum's distinctive designs. I have mostly replicated it as it was but some engineering was required for the straps. I believe they would have been originally machine knit in stockinette stitch and then folded. I opted for garter stitch with yoke-like decreasing to add shaping around the armholes. Soorik is intended to be worn over other clothing and a longer dress-length version is provided here. A few years ago, I came across a version of this smock at an exhibition on the island of Whalsay called Fair Isle Knitting Through The Decades. In that version, the pocket was centred and different motifs were used. As with other designs in this book, there are ways to add your own touch if desired!

Sizes:
1 (2, 3, 4, 5, 6, 7, 8)
Recommended to be worn with approx 5–10cm / 2–4" of positive ease at under bust.
See schematic key at the end of the pattern for full details.

Yarn (fingering / 4-ply-weight yarn in the following amounts):

Colourway 1
The model's height is 173cm / 5'8", with a chest circumference of 89cm / 35", and is wearing a size 1 (shorter version) shown in:
Jamieson & Smith 2ply Jumper Weight (fingering / 4-ply-weight; 100% Real Shetland Wool; 115m /125yds per 25g ball)
MC: Shade 80; 11 (13, 14, 15, 16, 17, 18, 20) balls
CC1: Shade 2; 2 balls
CC2: Shade 122; 1 ball
CC3: Shade FC38; 1 ball
CC4: Shade 125; 1 ball
CC5: Shade 1281; 1 ball
OR approx
MC: 1260 (1390, 1520, 1650, 1735, 1865, 1975, 2220)m / 1370 (1510, 1655, 1795, 1885, 2025, 2145, 2415)yds
CC1: 115 (115, 125, 125, 125, 145, 145, 145)m / 125 (125, 140, 140, 140, 160, 160, 160)yds
CC2, CC3, CC4 and CC5: 20 (20, 25, 25, 25, 25, 25, 25)m / 25 (25, 25, 25, 25, 30, 30, 30)yds each

Colourway 2
The model's height is 173cm / 5'8", with a chest circumference of 112cm / 44", and is wearing a size 3 (longer version) shown in:
Jamieson's of Shetland Spindrift (fingering / 4-ply-weight; 100% Shetland Wool; 105m / 115yds per 25g ball)
MC: Shaela; 16 (18, 19, 21, 22, 23, 25, 28) balls
CC1: Eesit; 2 balls
CC2: Artichoke; 1 ball
CC3: Bracken; 1 ball
CC4: Burnt Ochre; 1 ball
CC5: Scotch Broom; 1 ball
OR approx
MC: 1650 (1820, 1990, 2155, 2270, 2440, 2580, 2875)m / 1795 (1975, 2160, 2345, 2465, 2650, 2805, 3125)yds
CC1: 145 (145, 160, 160, 160, 185, 185, 185)m / 155 (155, 175, 175, 175, 200, 200, 200)yds
CC2, CC3, CC4 and CC5: 20 (20, 25, 25, 25, 25, 25, 25)m / 25 (25, 25, 25, 25, 30, 30, 30)yds each

Gauge:
24 sts & 34 rounds = 10cm / 4" over St st on 3.5mm needles after blocking

27 sts & 34 rounds = 10cm / 4" over Fair Isle Pattern on 3.5mm needles after blocking

25 sts & 48 rounds = 10cm / 4" over Garter Stitch on 3.25mm needles after blocking

Needles:
3.25mm / US 3 circular needle, 60cm / 24" and 80cm / 32" length or 100cm / 40" (for folded hem, top edge of Fair Isle bib and pockets, and shoulder straps)

3.5mm / US 4 circular needle, 80cm / 32" or 100cm / 40" length (for body)

3.5mm / US 4 circular needle, 40cm / 16" length (for Fair Isle bib)

3.5mm / US 4 DPNs or long circular (for working magic loop for pockets)

Always use a needle size that will result in the correct gauge after blocking.

Notions:
4 stitch markers (one of which should be unique for beg of round), waste yarn or stitch holder (for holding live sts), tapestry needle for weaving in ends

Notes:
This smock is worked in the round from the bottom up with a folded hem. Front and back are divided at the underarm and worked back and forth for the armhole shaping section. Steeks are then added to allow the Fair Isle bib to be worked in the round on both front and back simultaneously. Shoulder straps are picked up and knitted around the armholes, followed by two Fair Isle pockets that are worked in the round with steeks before being cut apart and sewn on to the body.

Stitch Glossary:
Garter Stitch (in the round)
Round 1: Knit.
Round 2: Purl.

PATTERN BEGINS

Hem
Using 3.25mm / US 3 circular needle, 80cm / 32" or 100cm / 40" length, MC and CC1, and using the two-colour long-tail method (see Special Techniques), cast on 274 (298, 322, 346, 362, 386, 406, 430) sts. Join for working in the round being careful not to twist. PM to indicate beg of round.

Using MC, work as folls:
Knit 20 rounds.
Change to 3.5mm / US 4 circular needle, 80cm / 32" or 100cm / 40" length.
Purl 1 round.
Knit 20 rounds.

Joining round: Fold the hem at the purl ridge bringing the cast-on edge with the contrasting yarn up behind the needles, to the inside of the work. Insert tip of LH needle into the first cast-on st (in the main colour and between the bumps of contrast colour) and knit it together with the first st on the needle. Continue knitting together 1 st from the cast-on edge together with the live sts until all sts have been joined.

Set-up round: P2, k133 (145, 157, 169, 177, 189, 199, 211), p2, PM (for side seam), p2, k to 2 sts before end of round, p2.
Round 1: Knit.
Round 2: *P2, k to 2 sts before next marker, p2, SM; rep from * once more. Repeating rounds 1–2, work a further 12 (12, 12, 12, 12, 12, 12, 20) rounds as set.
Dec round: *K3, k2tog, work to 5 sts before next marker, ssk, k3, SM; rep from * once more. *4 sts dec; 270 (294, 318, 343, 358, 382, 402, 426) sts rem.*

Short version
Repeating rounds 1–2, work dec round every 14th round a further 7 times. *28 sts dec; 242 (266, 290, 314, 330, 354, 374, 398) sts rem*
After last dec round work 7 more rounds in St st with G st seams.

Longer version
Repeating rounds 1–2, work dec round every 20th round a further 7 times. *28 sts dec; 242 (266, 290, 314, 330, 354, 374, 398) sts rem.*
After last dec round work 9 more rounds in St st with G st seams.

All versions
Next round: *K16 (20, 24, 28, 30, 34, 38, 42), (k2tog, k1) 12 times, k17 (21, 25, 29, 33, 37, 39, 43), (k2tog, k1) 12 times, k to side marker, SM; rep from * once more. *48 sts dec; 194 (218, 242, 266, 282, 306, 326, 350) sts rem.*

Divide Back and front
Next round: Work as set to 6 (8, 9, 11, 11, 11, 12, 14) sts past side seam marker (removing marker), place last 12 (16, 18, 22, 22, 22, 24, 28) sts worked onto waste yarn for underarm, work as set to end, place last 6 (8, 9, 11, 11, 11, 12, 14) sts worked and next 6 (8, 9, 11, 11, 11, 12, 14) sts from beg of round on waste yarn for underarm. *Two sets of 12 (16, 18, 22, 22, 22, 24, 28) sts set aside for underarms; 85 (93, 103, 111, 119, 131, 139, 147) sts rem for each back and front*
Break yarn.

Front
Now working flat / back and forth.
Rejoin MC to sts of front ready to begin a WS row.
**Purl 1 WS row.

Shape Armholes
Row 1 (RS): K1, ssk, k to last 3 sts, k2tog, k1. *2 sts dec*
Row 2 (WS): P1, p2tog tbl, p to last 3 sts, p2tog, p1. *2 sts dec*
Repeat the last 2 rows a further 7 (9, 10, 12, 14, 15, 17, 19) times and then work row 1 once more. *34 (42, 46, 54, 62, 66, 74, 82) sts dec; 51 (51, 57, 57, 57, 65, 65, 65) sts rem*

Work 5 (3, 3, 3, 3, 7, 7, 9) more rows in St st beginning and ending with a WS row.**
Leave yarn attached.

Back
Now working flat / back and forth.
Rejoin MC to sts of back ready to begin a WS row.
Work as for front from ** to **.
Break yarn.

Fair Isle Section
Round 1: With MC, 3.5mm / US 4 circular needle, 40cm / 16" length and starting where yarn is still attached to sts of front, knit across 51 (51, 57, 57, 57, 65, 65, 65) sts of front (chart row 1), PM, using the backwards-loop method (see Special Techniques), cast on 9 sts for steek, PM, knit across 51 (51, 57, 57, 57, 65, 65, 65) sts of back (chart row 1), PM, cast on 9 steek sts, PM to indicate beg of round. *102 (102, 114, 114, 114, 130, 130, 130) sts, plus 18 steek sts*

In the following section, use the shade guides for your chosen colourway in order to determine which yarn should be used for the background and pattern colours shown on the chart.

Round 2: *K1 in MC, work across row 2 of Chart A starting and ending as indicated for your size, k1 in MC, SM, (k1 in CC1, k1 in MC) 4 times, K1 in CC1, SM; rep from * once more.
Last round sets chart pattern, edge sts and steeks. Continue to work from Chart A until chart row 45 is complete, changing shades according to the shade guide for your chosen colourway.

Next round: Knit across sts of front in MC, cast off 9 steek sts, knit across sts of back, cast off 9 steek sts.
Change to 3.25mm / US 3 circular needle, 60cm / 24" long.
Continuing on front sts only and working flat in G st, knit 4 rows. Cast off all sts.

Still using 3.25mm / US 3 circular needle, 60cm / 24" long, re-join yarn to sts of back ready to begin a RS row. Knit 4 rows. Cast off all sts.

Cut steeks (see Special Techniques) before beginning armholes (do it one at a time).

Shoulder Straps (make two alike)
Note: *Pick up rate for sts is approx 3 out of 4 rows. It is important to pick up the correct number of sts. If your stitch count is off a little after pick up is complete, adjust to the correct number of sts by working decreases on the 2nd round worked.*
Using 3.25mm / US 3 circular needle, 80cm / 32" length, with RS facing, MC and starting at the center of the held underarm sts, knit across 6 (8, 9, 11, 11, 11, 12, 14) held underarm sts, pick up 16 (20, 21, 25, 28, 31, 34, 38) sts for the shaped underarm section to beg of Fair Isle section, then pick up and knit 36 sts along row ends for remainder of bib section (making sure to pick up inside the seam st worked in MC), turn work so that WS is facing and work a cable cast on (see Special Techniques) for 26 (26, 24, 24, 21, 24, 20, 20) sts, PM (for top of shoulder strap), cast on another 26 (26, 24, 24, 21, 24, 20, 20) sts, pick up and knit 36 sts on back bib section to end of Fair Isle, then 16 (20, 21, 25, 28, 31, 34, 38) sts for shaped underarm section and then knit across rem 6 (8, 9, 11, 11, 11, 12, 14) held underarm sts. *168 (180, 180, 192, 192, 204, 204, 216) sts total.*

Join for working in the round being careful not to twist. PM to indicate beg of round.

Beginning with a purl round work in G st in the round for 17 rounds (9 garter ridges), ending with a purl round.
Dec round: [K10, k2tog] to end of round. *14 (15, 15, 16, 16, 17, 17, 18) sts dec; 154 (165, 165, 176, 176, 187, 187, 198) sts rem.*
Work 5 more rounds in G st, beginning and ending with a purl round.
Dec round: [K9, k2tog] to end of round. *14 (15, 15, 16, 16, 17, 17, 18) sts dec; 140 (150, 150, 160, 160, 170, 170, 180) sts rem.*
Work 5 more rounds in G st beginning and ending with a purl round.
Cast off all sts.

Pockets

Note: *Pockets are worked together in the round and then steeked.*

Using 3.5mm / US 4 DPNs or long circular, with MC and the long-tail method, cast on 33 sts for pocket one, PM, for beg of steek, cast on 9 sts for steek, PM for end of steek, cast on 33 sts for pocket two, PM, cast on 9 sts for steek. Join for working in the round being careful not to twist. PM to indicate beg of round.

In the following section, use the shade guides for your chosen colourway in order to determine which yarn should be used for the background and pattern colours shown on the chart.

Round 1: *Work across row 1 of chart B, SM, [k1 in CC1, k1 in MC] 4 times, k1 in CC1, SM; rep from * once more.
Last round sets chart B and steeks. Continue to work as set until chart B row 34 is complete, changing shades according to the shade guide for your chosen colourway.

Next round: Using MC, knit across 33 sts of first pocket, cast off 9 steek sts, knit across sts of second pocket, cast off 9 steek sts.
Change to 3.25mm / US 3 circular needle, 60cm / 24" long.
Continuing on first pocket sts only and working flat in G st, knit 4 rows. Cast off all sts.
Still using 3.25mm / US 3 circular needle, 60cm / 24" long, re-join MC yarn to sts of second pocket ready to begin a RS row. Knit 4 rows. Cast off all sts.

FINISHING

Cut steeks.

It is recommended to block the garment and pockets separately and then sew the pockets on at the desired location. When sewing pockets it is helpful to use a piece of waste yarn in a contrast color to pick out the horizontal line you want the base of the pocket to match. *This is a very helpful tutorial for how to attach the pockets: youtu.be/1i-8ngp2SyM*

Weave in ends. Tack the cut steek edges to the WS of the garment using yarn. Block garment to schematic measurements. See Special Techniques for more blocking information.

SOORIK SCHEMATIC KEY

a. Hem circumference: 116 (126, 136.5, 146.5, 153, 163.5, 172, 182)cm / 45¾ (49¾, 53¾, 57¾, 60¼, 64¼, 67¾, 71¾)"

b. Under bust: 82 (92.5, 102.5, 112.5, 119.5, 129.5, 138, 148)m / 32¼ (36¼, 40¼, 44¼, 47, 51, 54¼, 58¼)"

c. Length to underarm (shorter version): 42.5 (42.5, 42.5, 42.5, 42.5, 42.5, 42.5, 45)cm / 16¾ (16¾, 16¾, 16¾, 16¾, 16¾, 16¾, 17¾)"

d. Length to underarm (longer version): 56 (56, 56, 56, 56, 56, 56, 58.5)cm / 22 (22, 22, 22, 22, 22, 22, 23)"

e. Cross shoulder (including straps): 31.5 (31.5, 33.5, 33.5, 33.5, 36.5, 36.5, 36.5)cm / 12½ (12½, 13¼, 13¼, 13¼, 14½, 14½, 14½)"

f. Armhole depth (taking into account straps): 29 (29.5, 29.5, 30.5, 30.5, 33.5, 33, 35)cm / 11½ (11½, 11½, 12, 12, 13¼, 13, 13¾)"

g. Neck drop: 10.5 (10.5, 10, 10, 8.5, 10, 8, 8)cm / 4¼ (4¼, 3¾, 3¾, 3¼, 3¾, 3¼, 3¼)"

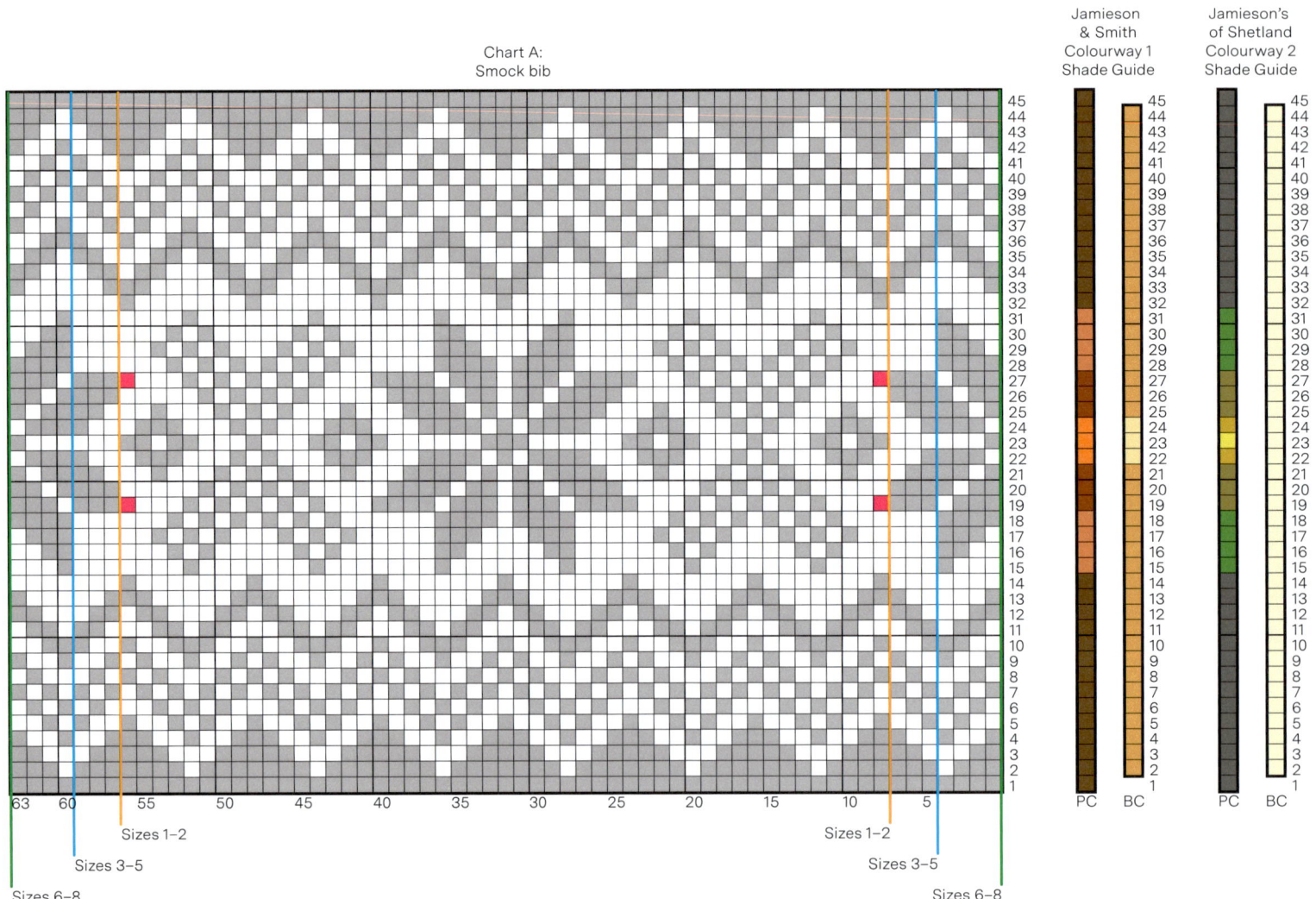

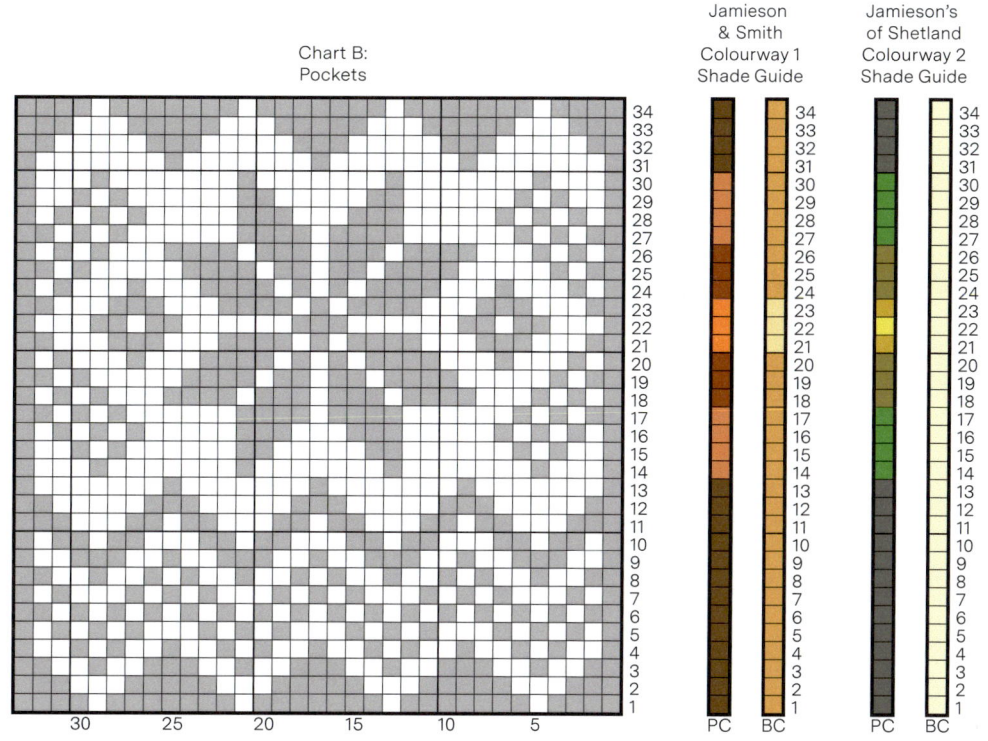

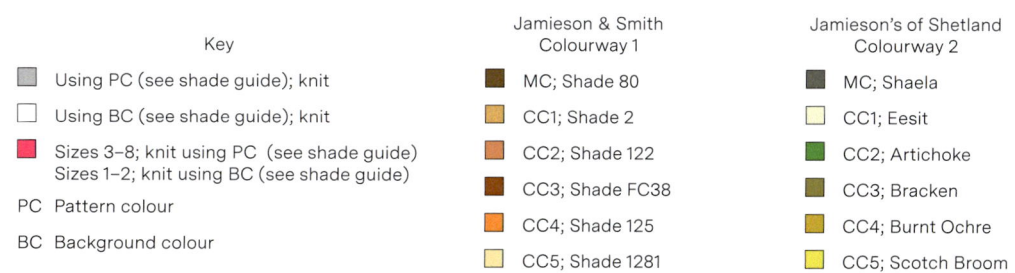

Elsk & Hjarta

Elsk

Elsk: *'to love' in Shetland dialect.*

Mum's collections included floor-length dresses and skirts with Fair Isle bands at the hem. I decided to combine some of these elements with others from different designs to come up with these dresses that are perhaps more accomplishable for a handknitter (the plain sections of her dresses would have been made on a knitting machine). Elsk and Hjarta are the same silhouette but with Fair Isle on one and Razor Shell Lace on the other.

Sizes:
1 (2, 3, 4, 5, 6, 7, 8, 9, 10)
Recommended to be worn with approx 0–2.5cm / 0–1" of negative ease. See schematic key at the end of the pattern for full details.

Yarn (fingering / 4-ply-weight yarn in the following amounts):

Note: *For crew neck version slightly less MC yarn will be required.*
MC: 1895 (2035, 2180, 2335, 2475, 2690, 2855, 3015, 3190, 3295)m / 2070 (2220, 2380, 2550, 2705, 2940, 3120, 3295, 3480, 3595)yds
CC1: 70 (75, 80, 80, 85, 95, 95, 100, 105, 105)m / 80 (80, 85, 90, 90, 105, 105, 110, 115, 115)yds
CC2: 95 (100, 105, 110, 115, 130, 130, 135, 140, 140)m / 105 (110, 115, 120, 125, 140, 145, 150, 155, 155)yds
CC3: 60 (65, 65, 70, 70, 80, 80, 85, 90, 90)m / 65 (70, 70, 75, 80, 85, 90, 95, 95, 95)yds
CC4: 25 (25, 25, 25, 30, 30, 30, 35, 35, 35)m / 25 (25, 30, 30, 30, 35, 35, 35, 35, 35)yds
CC5: 30 (30, 30, 30, 35, 35, 35, 40, 40, 40)m / 30 (30, 35, 35, 35, 40, 40, 40, 45, 45 yds

The model's height is 173cm / 5'8", with a chest circumference of 89cm / 35", and is wearing a size 2 (with turtle neck) shown in:
Jamieson & Smith Shetland Supreme Jumper Weight (fingering / 4-ply-weight; 100% Real Shetland Wool; 172m / 188yds per 50g ball)
MC: Shetland Black (2005); 11 (12, 13, 14, 15, 16, 17, 18, 19, 20) balls
CC1: Mooskit (2002); 1 ball
CC2: Moorit (2004); 1 ball
CC3: Shaela (2003); 1 ball
CC4: Gaulmogot (2006); 1 ball
CC5: Yuglet (2009); 1 ball

Gauge:
27 sts & 40 rounds = 10cm /4" over St st on 3.25mm needles after blocking

27 sts & 34 rounds = 10cm /4" over Fair Isle Pattern on 3.5mm needles after blocking

Needles:
3.25mm / US 3 circular needle, 80cm / 32" or 100cm / 40" length (for folded hem and body)

3.5mm / US 4 circular needle, 80cm / 32" or 100cm / 40" length (for body and yoke)

3.25mm / US 3 DPNs or long circular needle (if working magic loop for sleeves)

3.5mm / US 4 DPNs or long circular needle (if working magic loop for sleeves for Fair Isle band)

3mm / US 2 DPNs or long circular needle (if working magic loop for sleeves for cuff)

3.25mm / US 3 circular needle, 40cm / 16" length (for neckband)

3.5mm / US 4 circular needle, 40cm / 16" length (for neckband, turtleneck version only)

Always use a needle size that will result in the correct gauge after blocking

Notions:
4 stitch markers (one of which should be unique for beg of round), 2 locking stitch markers, waste yarn or stitch holder (for holding live sts), tapestry needle for weaving in ends

Notes:
This dress is worked in the round from the bottom up. The dress starts with a folded hem and Fair Isle band, before decreases are worked to shape the skirt. The body is then divided at underarm from which point the front and back are worked back and forth, separately. The balloon-shaped sleeves are worked top down after picking up stitches around the armhole and the sleeve cap is shaped with short rows. The sleeves feature a Fair Isle band at the widest point. There is a choice of crew neck or turtleneck to complete the neck.

Stitch Glossary:
2x2 Rib (in the round):
Round 1: [K2, p2] to end.
Rep round 1 for pattern.

Abbreviations:
wrap and turn: See Special Techniques on page 143.

A full list of abbreviations appears on page 145.

PATTERN BEGINS

Hem
Using 3.25mm / US 3 circular needle, 80cm / 32" or 100cm / 40" length, MC and CC1, and using the two-colour long-tail cast-on method (see Special Techniques), cast on 264 (288, 312, 336, 360, 384, 408, 432, 456, 456) sts.
Join for working in the round being careful not to twist. PM to indicate beg of round.

Using MC work as folls:
Knit 20 rounds.
Change to 3.5mm / US 4 circular needle, 80cm / 32" or 100cm / 40" length.
Purl 1 round.
Knit 20 rounds

Joining round: Fold the hem at the purl ridge bringing the cast-on edge with the contrasting yarn up behind the needles, to the inside of the work. Insert tip of LH needle into the first cast-on stitch (in the main colour and between the bumps of contrast colour) and knit it together with the first stitch on the needle. Continue knitting together 1 stitch from the cast-on edge together with the live stitches until all sts have been joined.

Continue using 3.5mm / US 4 circular needle, 80cm / 32" or 100cm / 40" length.
Round 1: Reading from right to left, work across row 1 of Chart A for your size, starting and ending where indicated for your size, repeating marked section 10 (11, 12, 12, 14, 15, 16, 16, 18, 18) times in total. Last round sets chart pattern. Continue to work from chart, changing yarns as indicated, until chart row 41 is complete.

Change to 3.25mm / US 3 circular needle, 80cm / 32" or 100cm / 40" length.
Set-up round: K131 (144, 155, 168, 179, 192, 203, 216, 227, 228), PM for side seam, k to end.

Sizes 1, 3, 5, 7 and 9 only
Dec round: *K2tog, k to marker, SM; rep from * once more. *2 sts dec; 262 (–, 310, –, 358, –, 406, –, 454, –) sts rem*

All Sizes
Dec round: *K3, k2tog, work to 5 sts before next marker, ssk, k3, SM; rep from * once more. *4 sts dec; 258 (284, 306, 332, 354, 380, 402, 428, 450, 452) sts rem*

Work dec round every 16th (16th, 16th, 16th, 16th, 16th, 16th, –, –, 18th) round 10 (8, 8, 5, 5, 3, 3, 0, 0, 9) times, then every 12th round 0 (3, 3, 7, 7, 10, 10, 14, 14, 0) times. *40 (44, 44, 48, 48, 52, 52, 56, 56, 36) sts dec; 218 (240, 262, 284, 306, 328, 350, 372, 394, 416) sts rem*

After last dec round work 28 (25, 24, 25, 24, 21, 20, 21, 20, 27) more plain rounds, ending 8 (10, 11, 12, 13, 14, 15, 16, 17, 18) sts before beg of the round marker on final round. If row tension is correct in both St st and Fair Isle patterns, body will measure 66.5cm / 26" from hem.

Divide Back and Fronts
Next round: K next 16 (20, 22, 24, 26, 28, 30, 32, 34, 36) sts (removing marker), then transfer these sts to waste yarn for underarm, k to 8 (10, 11, 12, 13, 14, 15, 16, 17, 18) sts before next side seam marker, place 93 (100, 109, 118, 127, 136, 145, 154, 163, 172) sts of front just knitted onto waste yarn, k next 16 (20, 22, 24, 26, 28, 30, 32, 34, 36) sts (removing marker) then transfer these 16 (20, 22, 24, 26, 28, 30, 32, 34, 36) sts to waste yarn for underarm, k to end. *Two sets of 16 (20, 22, 24, 26, 28, 30, 32, 34, 36) underarm sts and one set of 93 (100, 109, 118, 127, 136, 145, 154, 163, 172) front sts are set aside; 93 (100, 109, 118, 127, 136, 145, 154, 163, 172) sts rem for back*

Back
**Continuing where yarn is attached work as folls:
Next row (WS): P93 (100, 109, 118, 127, 136, 145, 154, 163, 172) sts of back.

Read the following dec row instructions, but do NOT work them. Work armhole dec rows as described for your size below.
Double dec row: K1, sssk, k to 4 sts before end, k3tog, k1. *4 sts dec*
Single dec row: K1, ssk, k to 3 sts before end, k2tog, k1. *2 sts dec*

Sizes 1–2: Work a single dec row every RS row 5 (7, –, –, –, –, –, –, –, –) times. *10 (14 –, –, –, –, –, –, –, –, –) sts dec; 83 (86, –, –, –, –, –, –, –, –) back sts rem*
Sizes 3–10: Work a double dec row every RS row – (–, 3, 4, 5, 6, 7, 7, 8, 9) times, then work a single dec row every RS row – (–, 5, 6, 5, 5, 5, 5, 6, 7) times. *– (–, 22, 28, 30, 34, 38, 38, 44, 50) sts dec; – (–, 87, 90, 97, 102, 107, 116, 119, 122) back sts rem*

All Sizes
****Continue in St st for a further 63 (61, 63, 63, 65, 65, 67, 69, 69, 69) rows, beginning and ending with a WS row.

Shape Back Shoulders
Short row 1 (RS): K to last 7 (7, 7, 7, 8, 8, 8, 9, 9, 9) sts, wrap and turn.
Short row 2 (WS): P to last 7 (7, 7, 7, 8, 8, 8, 9, 9, 9) sts, wrap and turn.
Short row 3: K to 6 (6, 7, 7, 7, 8, 8, 9, 9, 9) sts before prev wrapped st, wrap and turn.
Short row 4: P to 6 (6, 7, 7, 7, 8, 8, 9, 9, 9) sts before prev wrapped st, wrap and turn.
Next row (RS): K to end, working wraps together with wrapped sts.
Next row (WS): P19 (19, 20, 20, 22, 23, 24, 26, 27, 27), cast off 45 (48, 47, 50, 53, 56, 59, 64, 65, 68) sts, p to end, working wraps together with wrapped sts.
Transfer both sets of 19 (19, 20, 20, 22, 23, 24, 26, 27, 27) shoulder sts to separate lengths of waste yarn.

Front
Reattach yarn to held sts of front ready to begin a WS row and work as for Back from ** to **. *83 (86, 87, 90, 97, 102, 107, 116, 119, 122) front sts*

All Sizes
Continue in St st for a further 41 (37, 39, 37, 39, 39, 41, 41, 41, 39) rows, beginning and ending with a WS row.

Shape Front Neck
Front neck cast-off row (RS): K26 (27, 28, 29, 32, 33, 35, 38, 38, 39) sts, join new ball of yarn and cast off centre 31 (32, 31, 32, 33, 36, 37, 40, 43, 44) sts for front neck, k to end. *26 (27, 28, 29, 32, 33, 35, 38, 38, 39) sts rem for both left and right fronts*
Working right and left front separately now.

Right Front
Continuing where yarn is attached p across one WS row.
Neck dec row (RS): K1, ssk, k to end. *1 st dec; 25 (26, 27, 28, 31, 32, 34, 37, 37, 38) sts rem*
Continue in St st and rep neck dec row every RS row a further 6 (7, 7, 8, 9, 9, 10, 11, 10, 11) times. *19 (19, 20, 20, 22, 23, 24, 26, 27, 27) sts rem*

Continue in St st for another 7 (7, 7, 7, 5, 5, 3, 3, 5, 5) rows beginning and ending with a WS row.

Shape Right Front Shoulder
Short row 1 (RS): K to last 7 (7, 7, 7, 8, 8, 8, 9, 9, 9) sts, wrap and turn.
Short row 2 (WS): P to neck edge, turn.
Short row 3: K to 6 (6, 7, 7, 7, 8, 8, 9, 9, 9) sts before prev wrapped st, wrap and turn.
Short row 4: P to neck edge, turn.
Next row (RS): K to end, working wraps together with wrapped sts
Next row (WS): Purl.
Break yarn.
Transfer 19 (19, 20, 20, 22, 23, 24, 26, 27, 27) right shoulder sts to waste yarn.

Left Front
Continuing where yarn is attached p across one WS row.
Neck dec row (RS): K to last 3 sts of row, k2tog, k1. *1 st dec; 25 (26, 27, 28, 31, 32, 34, 37, 37, 38) sts rem*
Continue in St st and rep neck dec row every RS row a further 6 (7, 7, 8, 9, 9, 10, 11, 10, 11) times. *19 (19, 20, 20, 22, 23, 24, 26, 27, 27) sts rem*

Continue in St st for another 8 (8, 8, 8, 6, 6, 4, 4, 6, 6) rows beginning with a WS row and ending with a RS row.

Shape Left Front Shoulder
Short row 1 (WS): P to 7 (7, 7, 7, 8, 8, 8, 9, 9, 9) sts before end of row, wrap and turn.
Short row 2: K to neck edge, turn.
Short row 3: P to 6 (6, 7, 7, 7, 8, 8, 9, 9, 9) sts before prev wrapped st, wrap and turn.
Short row 4: K to neck edge, turn.
Next row (WS): P to end, working wraps together with wrapped sts.
Break yarn.

Join the shoulders with a three-needle cast off as folls:
Turn the knitting to the WS and return the left back shoulder sts to needles. Hold the left front shoulder sts parallel with the left back shoulder sts. Using a third needle and working from the armhole edge to the neck edge knit together the first st from the front needle with the first st on the rear needle. *Knit together the next st from the front and rear needles. Cast off one st on the right needle tip as normal. Repeat from * until all sts have been joined and cast off.

Repeat this process for the right front and back shoulder sts.

SLEEVES
Count 12 (12, 12, 14, 14, 14, 14, 16, 16, 16) rows down from the shoulder seam on each side of the armhole and place a locking marker in the 13th (13th, 13th, 15th, 15th, 15th, 15th, 17th, 17th, 17th) row.

With RS facing, using MC yarn and 3.25mm / US 3 DPNs or long circular needle, and beginning at the shoulder seam, pick up and knit 1 st at the shoulder join, PM, pick up and knit 9 (9, 9, 10, 10, 10, 10, 12, 12, 12) sts to marker, 26 (27, 29, 30, 31, 32, 34, 34, 37, 39) sts to bottom of armhole, k7 (9, 10, 11, 12, 13, 14, 15, 16, 17) along underarm sts, PM, k2tog (this will be the centre underarm st), PM, k7 (9, 10, 11, 12, 13, 14, 15, 16, 17) sts along remainder of underarm sts, pick up and knit 26 (27, 29, 30, 31, 32, 34, 34, 37, 39) sts to marker, pick up and knit 9 (9, 10, 10, 10, 10, 10, 12, 12, 12) sts to shoulder seam. Pm for beg of round. *86 (92, 98, 104, 108, 112, 118, 124, 132, 138) sts total (2 seam sts with markers either side at top of shoulder and centre underarm. Locking markers can now be removed).*

Shape Sleeve Cap
Note: *Cap is shaped using the Wrap & Turn method of short rows. Do not pick up wraps for this section.*
Short row 1 (RS): K1 (centre shoulder st), SM, k9 (9, 9, 10, 10, 10, 10, 12, 12, 12), wrap and turn.
Short row 2 (WS): P19 (19, 19, 21, 21, 21, 21, 25, 25, 25) (going past centre shoulder st) wrap and turn.
Short row 3: K to prev wrapped st, k wrapped st, k1, wrap and turn.
Short row 4: P to prev wrapped st, p wrapped st, p1, wrap and turn.
Short rows 5–6: Repeat short rows 3–4 once more.
Short row 7: K to prev wrapped st, k wrapped st, wrap and turn.
Short row 8: P to prev wrapped st, p wrapped st, wrap and turn.
Repeat short rows 7 and 8 a further 14 (14, 16, 17, 18, 19, 21, 21, 24, 26) times, at which point there will be 13 (16, 17, 18, 19, 20, 21, 22, 23, 24) sts rem unworked before the centre underarm marker on each side.

Note: *In the next section you will wrap 2 sts with every turn. Work the same as a single wrap and turn but slip 2 sts together instead of 1.*
Short row 1: K to prev wrapped st, k wrapped st, wrap 2 sts and turn.
Short row 2: P to prev wrapped st, p wrapped st, wrap 2 sts and turn.
Short row 3: K to prev wrapped sts, k2tog, wrap 2 sts and turn. *1 st dec*
Short row 4: P to prev wrapped sts, p2tog, wrap 2 sts and turn. *1 st dec; 84 (90, 96, 102, 106, 110, 116, 122, 130, 136) sts*

Sizes 2–10 only
Short rows 5–6: Repeat short rows 3–4 once more. *2 sts dec; – (88, 94, 100, 104, 108, 114, 120, 128, 134) sts*

All sizes
Note: *The final pair of short rows only wraps a single stitch each time.*
Next short row: K to prev wrapped sts, k2tog, wrap 1 st and turn. *1 st dec*
Next short row: P to prev wrapped sts, p2tog, wrap 1 st and turn. *1 st dec; 82 (86, 92, 98, 102, 106, 112, 118, 126, 132) sts*
Next row (RS): K to beg of round marker.

Shape sleeve
Begin working in the round.
Next round: K to prev wrapped st, k2tog, k to 1 st before next wrapped st, k2tog, k to end. *2 sts dec; 80 (84, 90, 96, 100, 104, 110, 116, 124, 130) sts rem*

The beg of the round is now moved to the underside of the arm. You will essentially swap the placement of the BOR marker and second marker (still keeping two markers total in place):
Partial round: Make sure that the beg of round marker at top of shoulder now becomes the second marker, k40 (42, 45, 48, 50, 52, 55, 58, 62, 65), replace beg of round marker at the underarm.

Continue to work St st in the round until sleeve measures 5 (6.5, 7.5, 10, 12.5, 14, 14, 14, 14, 14) cm / 2 (2½, 3, 4, 5, 5½, 5½, 5½, 5½, 5½)" from underarm.
Inc round: *K1, SM, k2, M1L, k to 2 sts before next marker, M1R, k2, SM; rep from * once more. *4 sts inc*

Knit 9 (9, 10, 12, 13, 5, 5, 8, 11, 16) rounds. Repeat last 10 (10, 11, 13, 14, 6, 6, 9, 12, 17) rounds a further 8 (7, 6, 4, 3, 8, 7, 5, 3, 2) times. *36 (32, 28, 20, 16, 36, 32, 24, 16, 12) sts inc; 116 (116, 118, 116, 116, 140, 142, 140, 140, 142) sts*

Sizes 1, 2, 4, 5, 6, 8 and 9 only
Work inc round once more. *4 sts inc; 120 (120, –, 120, 120, 144, –, 144, 144, –) sts*

Sizes 3, 7 and 10 only
Inc round: *K1, SM, k2, M1L, k to next marker, SM; rep from * once more. *2 sts inc; – (–, 120, –, –, –, 144, –, –, 144) sts*
You can now remove the second marker.

All sizes
Knit 0 (5, 3, 5, 4, 1, 7, 1, 7, 4) rounds.
Change to 3.5mm / US 4 DPNs or long circular needle.
Round 1: Work across 24 sts from marked pattern repeat section of row 1 of Chart A 5 (5, 5, 5, 5, 6, 6, 6, 6, 6) times.
Last round sets chart pattern. Continue to work from chart, changing yarns as indicated, until chart row 41 is complete.

Change to 3.25mm / US 3 DPNs or long circular needle.
Knit 6 rounds straight using MC. If row tension is correct, sleeve now measures 41.5cm / 16½" from underarm.
Dec round: [K2tog] to end. *60 (60, 60, 60, 60, 72, 72, 72, 72, 72) sts dec; 60 (60, 60, 60, 60, 72, 72, 72, 72, 72) sts rem*

Sizes 1–3
Dec round: *K13, k2tog; rep from * to end.
4 sts dec; 56 sts rem

Sizes 4 and 5
Next round: Knit.

Sizes 6–10
Dec round: *K– (–, –, –, –, 7, 7, 7, 16, 16), k2tog; rep from * to end. *– (–, –, –, –, 8, 8, 8, 4, 4) sts dec; – (–, –, –, –, 64, 64, 64, 68, 68) sts rem*

All sizes
Change to 3mm / US 2 DPNs or long circular needle.
Work in 2x2 Rib until cuff measures 10cm / 4".
Cast off all sts in rib.

FINISHING
Neckband
Using 3.25mm / US 3 circular needle, 40cm / 16" length, MC, and starting at the right shoulder join, with RS facing, pick up and knit 45 (48, 47, 50, 53, 56, 59, 64, 65, 68) back neck sts, then pick up and knit 14 (16, 17, 19, 19, 20, 20, 22, 22, 22) sts to front neck sts, pick up and knit 31 (32, 31, 32, 33, 36, 37, 40, 43, 44) cast-off front neck sts, then pick up and knit 14 (16, 17, 19, 19, 20, 20, 22, 22, 22) sts to left shoulder join. *104 (112, 112, 120, 124, 132, 136, 148, 152, 156) sts*
Join for working in the round and PM to indicate beg of round.

Crew neck
Work in 2x2 Rib for 5 rounds then cast off all sts in rib pattern being careful not to cast off too tightly.

Turtleneck
Work in 2x2 Rib until neckband measures 10cm / 4". Change to 3.5mm / US 4 circular needle, 40cm / 16" length and continue in rib pattern for another 11.5cm / 4½". Cast off all sts in rib pattern being careful not to cast off too tightly.

Weave in ends. Block garment to schematic measurements. See Special Techniques for detailed blocking information.

ELSK SCHEMATIC KEY

a. Hem circumference: 99.5 (108.5, 117.5, 126.5, 135.5, 144.5, 153.5, 162.5, 171.5, 171.5)cm / 39 (42¾, 46¼, 49¾, 53¼, 57, 60½, 64, 67½, 67½)"

b. Bust circumference: 82 (90.5, 98.5, 107, 115, 123.5, 131.5, 140, 148.5, 156.5)cm / 32¼ (35½, 38¾, 42, 45¼, 48½, 51¾, 55, 58¼, 61¾)"

c. Length to underarm: 66.5cm / 26"

d. Armhole depth: 19 (19.5, 20.5, 21.5, 22, 22.5, 23.5, 24, 25, 26)cm / 7½ (7¾, 8, 8½, 8¾, 9, 9¼, 9½, 10, 10¼)"

e. Cross shoulder: 31 (32.5, 32.5, 34, 36.5, 38.5, 40.5, 43.5, 45, 46)cm / 12¼ (12¾, 13, 13¼, 14¼, 15, 15¾, 17¼, 17¾, 18)"

f. Neck drop: 5.5 (6, 6, 6.5, 6.5, 6.5, 6.5, 7, 7, 7.5)cm / 2 (2¼, 2¼, 2½, 2½, 2½, 2½, 2¾, 2¾, 3)"

g. Back neck width: 17 (18, 17.5, 19, 20, 21, 22, 24, 24.5, 25.5)cm / 6¾ (7, 7, 7½, 7¾, 8¼, 8¾, 9½, 9¾, 10)"

h. Upper arm circumference: 30 (31.5, 34, 36, 37.5, 39, 41.5, 43.5, 46.5, 49)cm / 11¾ (12½, 13¼, 14¼, 14¾, 15½, 16¼, 17¼, 18¼, 19¼)"

i. Balloon sleeve wrist circumference: 21 (21, 21, 22.5, 22.5, 24, 24, 24, 25.5, 25.5)cm / 8¼ (8¼, 8¼, 9, 9, 9½, 9½, 9½, 10, 10)"

j. Balloon sleeve circumference at widest point: 45 (45, 45, 45, 45, 54, 54, 54, 54, 54)cm / 17¾ (17¾, 17¾, 17¾, 17¾, 21¼, 21¼, 21¼, 21¼, 21¼)"

k. Balloon sleeve length from underarm incl. ribbing: 52.5cm / 20¾"

Chart A

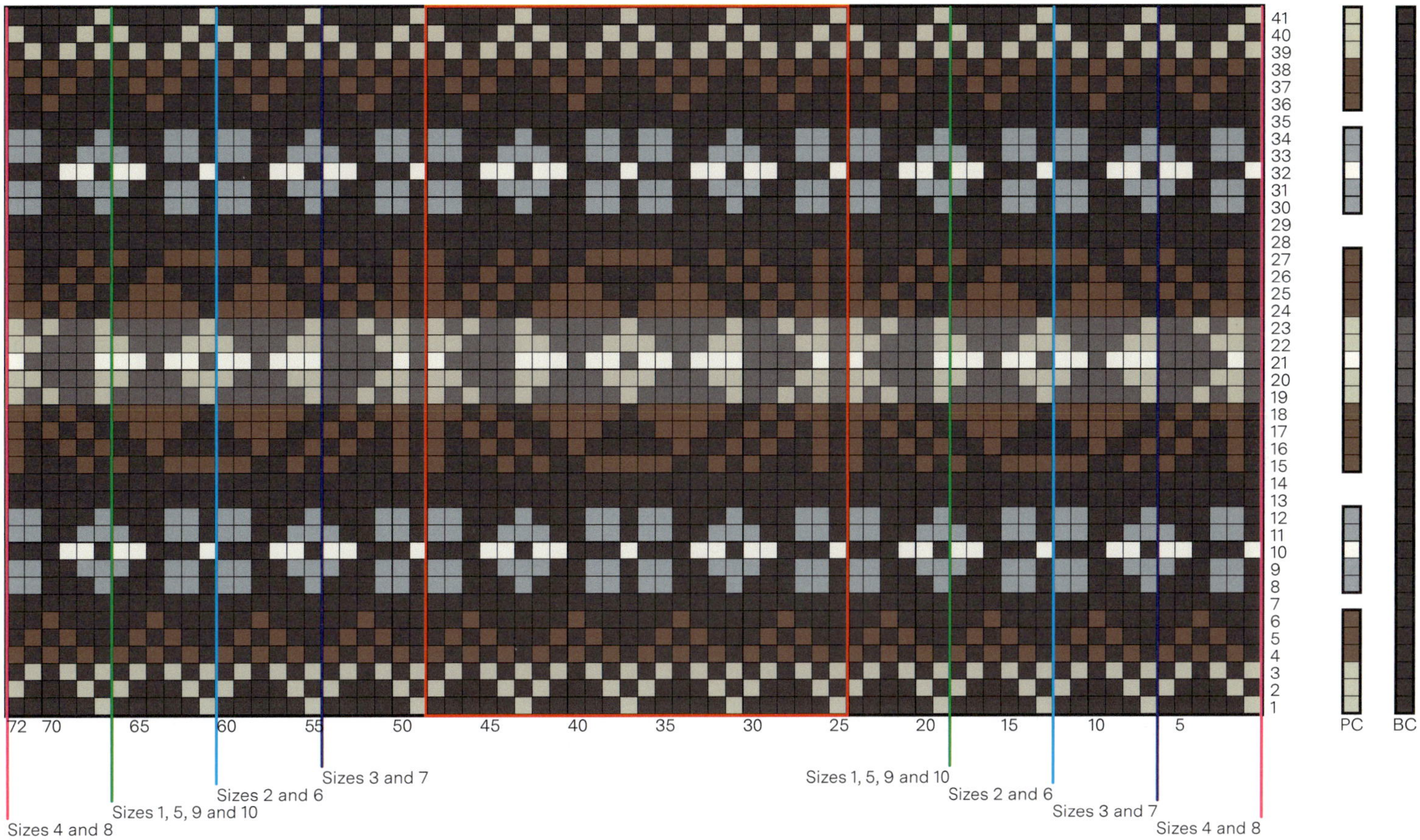

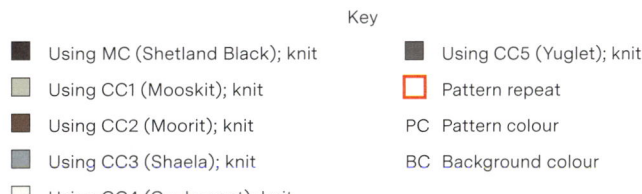

Key

- Using MC (Shetland Black); knit
- Using CC1 (Mooskit); knit
- Using CC2 (Moorit); knit
- Using CC3 (Shaela); knit
- Using CC4 (Gaulmogot); knit
- Using CC5 (Yuglet); knit
- Pattern repeat
- PC Pattern colour
- BC Background colour

Hjarta

Hjarta: *'darling' or 'sweetheart' in Shetland dialect.*

This dress is a partner to Elsk. The same overall shape is used but instead of Fair Isle at the hem and cuffs I have used the Razor Shell Lace pattern. Although this version is shown with a crew neck, there are instructions for adding a turtleneck if you prefer.

Sizes:
1 (2, 3, 4, 5, 6, 7, 8, 9, 10)
Recommended to be worn with approx 0–2.5cm / 0–1" of negative ease. See schematic key at the end of the pattern for full details.

Yarn (fingering / 4-ply-weight yarn in the following amounts):

Note: *For the turtleneck version slightly more yarn will be required.*
MC: 1770 (1895, 2035, 2210, 2335, 2470, 2645, 2785, 2945, 3100)m / 1935 (2070, 2225, 2415, 2555, 2700, 2895, 3045, 3220, 3390)yds
CC1: 220 (230, 235, 255, 265, 270, 290, 300, 305, 315)m / 240 (250, 255, 275, 285, 295, 315, 325, 335, 340)yds
CC2: 80 (80, 85, 90, 95, 95, 105, 105, 110, 110)m / 85 (90, 90, 100, 100, 105, 110, 115, 120, 120)yds
CC3: 155 (160, 165, 180, 185, 190, 205, 210, 215, 220)m / 165 (175, 180, 195, 200, 205, 220, 225, 235, 240)yds

The model's height is 173cm / 5'8", with a chest circumference of 112cm / 44", and is wearing a size 5 (with crew neck) shown in:
Jamieson & Smith Shetland Supreme Jumper Weight (fingering / 4-ply-weight; 100% Real Shetland Wool; 172m / 188yds per 50g ball)
MC: Mooskit (2002); 11 (11, 12, 13, 14, 15, 16, 17, 18, 19) balls
and
Jamieson & Smith 2ply Jumper Weight (fingering / 4-ply-weight; 100% Real Shetland Wool; 115m / 125yds per 25g ball)
CC1: Shade FC46; 2 (2, 3, 3, 3, 3, 3, 3, 3, 3) balls
CC2: Shade 54; 1 ball
CC3: Shade 32; 2 balls

Gauge:
27 sts & 40 rounds = 10cm / 4" over St st on 3.25mm needles after blocking

27 sts & 34 rounds = 10cm / 4" over Razor Shell Pattern on 3.5mm needles after blocking

Needles:
3.25mm / US 3 circular needle, 80cm / 32" or 100cm / 40" length (for folded hem and body)

3.5mm / US 4 circular needle, 80cm / 32" or 100cm / 40" length (for body and yoke)

3.25mm / US 3 DPNs or long circular needle (if working magic loop for sleeves)

3.5mm / US 4 DPNs or long circular needle (if working magic loop for sleeves for Razor Shell band)

3mm / US 2 DPNs or long circular needle (if working magic loop for sleeves for cuff)

3.25mm / US 3 circular needle, 40cm / 16" length (for neckband)

3.5mm / US 4 circular needle, 40cm / 16" length (for neckband, turtle neck version only)

Always use a needle size that will result in the correct gauge after blocking.

Notions:
4 stitch markers (one of which should be unique for beg of round), 2 locking stitch markers, waste yarn or stitch holder (for holding live sts), tapestry needle for weaving in ends

Notes:
This dress is worked in the round from the bottom up. The dress starts with a folded hem and Striped Razor Shell band, before decreases are worked to shape the skirt. The body is then divided at underarm from which point the front and back are worked back and forth, separately. The balloon-shaped sleeves are worked top down after picking up stitches around the armhole and the sleeve cap is shaped with short rows. The sleeves feature a Razor Shell band at the widest point. There is a choice of crew neck or turtle neck to complete the neck.

Stitch Glossary:
Stripe Sequence (also shown on chart)
Rounds 1–2: CC1
Rounds 3–4: MC
Rounds 5–8: CC1
Rounds 9–10: CC2
Rounds 11–12: CC1
Rounds 13–16: CC2
Rounds 17–18: CC3
Rounds 19–20: CC2
Rounds 21–22: MC
Rounds 23–24: CC3
Rounds 25–26: CC1
Rounds 27–28: CC3
Rounds 29–30: MC
Rounds 31–32: CC2
Rounds 33–34: CC3
Rounds 35–38: CC2
Rounds 39–40: CC1
Rounds 41–42: CC2
Rounds 43–46: CC1
Rounds 47–48: MC
Rounds 49–50: CC1
Rounds 51–52: MC

Razor Shell Pattern (in the round):
Round 1: [Yo, k3, sk2po, k3, yo, k1] to end.
Round 2: Purl.
Rep rounds 1–2 for pattern.

2x2 Rib (in the round):
Round 1: [K2, p2] to end.
Rep round 1 for pattern.

Abbreviations:
wrap and turn: See Special Techniques on page 143.

A full list of abbreviations appears on page 145.

PATTERN BEGINS

Using 3.25mm / US 3 circular needle, 80cm / 32" or 100cm / 40" length, MC and CC1, and using the two-colour long-tail cast-on method (see Special Techniques), cast on 260 (280, 300, 320, 340, 360, 380, 400, 420, 440) sts.
Join for working in the round being careful not to twist. PM to indicate beg of round.

Using MC only, work as folls:
Knit 20 rounds.
Change to 3.5mm / US 4 circular needle, 80cm / 32" or 100cm / 40" length.
Purl 1 round.
Knit 20 rounds.

Joining round: Fold the hem at the purl ridge bringing the cast-on edge with the contrasting yarn up behind the needles, to the inside of the work. Insert tip of LH needle into the first cast-on stitch (in the main colour and between the bumps of contrast colour) and knit it together with the first stitch on the needle. Continue knitting together 1 stitch from the cast-on edge together with the live stitches until all sts have been joined.

Continue using 3.5mm / US 4 circular needle, 80cm / 32" or 100cm / 40" length and MC.
Set-up round: Purl.

Now work from the Stripe Sequence pattern starting at row 1 with CC1, and work pattern as folls:
Round 1: [Yo, k3, sk2po, k3, yo, k1] 26 (28, 30, 32, 34, 36, 38, 40, 42, 44) times.
Round 2: P to end.
Last 2 rounds set Razor Shell Pattern. Continue in Razor Shell Pattern changing colours as indicated, until Stripe Sequence row 52 is complete.

Change to 3.25mm / US 3 circular needle, 80cm / 32" or 100cm / 40" length, and working in St st using MC only, work as folls:
Set-up round: K129 (140, 149, 160, 169, 180, 189, 200, 209, 220), PM for side seam, k to end.

Sizes 1, 3, 5, 7, and 9 only
Dec round: *K2tog, k to marker, SM; rep from * once more. *2 sts dec; 258 (–, 298, –, 338, –, 378, –, 418, –) sts rem*

All Sizes
Dec round: *K3, k2tog, work to 5 sts before next marker, ssk, k3, SM; rep from * once more. *4 sts dec; 254 (276, 294, 316, 334, 356, 374, 396, 414, 436) sts rem*
Work dec round every 20th (20th, 24th, 24th, 24th, 24th, 28th, 28th, 32nd, 32nd) round 3 (3, 4, 4, 5, 5, 4, 4, 5, 5) times, then every 16th (16th, 16th, 16th, 18th, 18th, 24th, 24th, –, –) round 6 (6, 4, 4, 2, 2, 2, 2, –, –) times. *36 (36, 32, 32, 28, 28, 24, 24, 20, 20) sts dec; 218 (240, 262, 284, 306, 328, 350, 372, 394, 416) sts rem*

After last dec round work a further 24 (24, 20, 20, 24, 24, 20, 20, 20, 20) rounds in St st, ending 8 (10, 11, 12, 13, 14, 15, 16, 17, 18) sts before beg of the round marker on final round. If row tension in St st and Razor Shell Patterns are correct then body should measure 67.5cm / 26½" from hem.

Divide Back and Fronts
Next round: K next 16 (20, 22, 24, 26, 28, 30, 32, 34, 36) sts (removing marker), then transfer these sts to waste yarn for underarm, k to 8 (10, 11, 12, 13, 14, 15, 16, 17, 18) sts before next side seam marker, place 93 (100, 109, 118, 127, 136, 145, 154, 163, 172) sts of front just knitted onto waste yarn, k next 16 (20, 22, 24, 26, 28, 30, 32, 34, 36) sts (removing marker) then transfer these 16 (20, 22, 24, 26, 28, 30, 32, 34, 36) sts to waste yarn for underarm, k to end. *Two sets of 16 (20, 22, 24, 26, 28, 30, 32, 34, 36) underarm sts and one set of 93 (100, 109, 118, 127, 136, 145, 154, 163, 172) front sts are set aside; 93 (100, 109, 118, 127, 136, 145, 154, 163, 172) sts rem for back*

Back
**Continuing where yarn is attached work as folls:
Next row (WS): P93 (100, 109, 118, 127, 136, 145, 154, 163, 172) sts of back.

Read the following dec row instructions, but do NOT work them. Work armhole dec rows as described for your size below.
Double dec row: K1, sssk, k to 4 sts before end, k3tog, k1. *4 sts dec*
Single dec row: K1, ssk, k to 3 sts before end, k2tog, k1. *2 sts dec*

Sizes 1–2: Work a single dec row every RS row 5 (7, –, –, –, –, –, –, –, –) times. *10 (14 –, –, –, –, –, –, –, –) sts dec; 83 (86, –, –, –, –, –, –, –, –) back sts rem*
Sizes 3–10: Work a double dec row every RS row – (–, 3, 4, 5, 6, 7, 7, 8, 9) times, then work a single dec row every RS row – (–, 5, 6, 5, 5, 5, 5, 6, 7) times. *– (–, 22, 28, 30, 34, 38, 38, 44, 50) sts dec; – (–, 87, 90, 97, 102, 107, 116, 119, 122) back sts rem*

All Sizes
**Continue in St st for a further 63 (61, 63, 63, 65, 65, 67, 69, 69, 69) rows, beginning and ending with a WS row.

Shape Back Shoulders
Short row 1 (RS): K to last 7 (7, 7, 7, 8, 8, 8, 9, 9, 9) sts, wrap and turn.
Short row 2 (WS): P to last 7 (7, 7, 7, 8, 8, 8, 9, 9, 9) sts, wrap and turn.
Short row 3: K to 6 (6, 7, 7, 7, 8, 8, 9, 9, 9) sts before prev wrapped st, wrap and turn.
Short row 4: P to 6 (6, 7, 7, 7, 8, 8, 9, 9, 9) sts before prev wrapped st, wrap and turn.
Next row (RS): K to end, working wraps together with wrapped sts.
Next row (WS): P19 (19, 20, 20, 22, 23, 24, 26, 27, 27), cast off 45 (48, 47, 50, 53, 56, 59, 64, 65, 68) sts, p to end, working wraps together with wrapped sts.
Transfer both sets of 19 (19, 20, 20, 22, 23, 24, 26, 27, 27) shoulder sts to separate lengths of waste yarn.

Front
Re-join MC yarn to held sts of front ready to begin a WS row and work as for Back from ** to **. *83 (86, 87, 90, 97, 102, 107, 116, 119, 122) front sts*

All Sizes
Continue in St st for a further 41 (37, 39, 37, 39, 39, 41, 41, 41, 39) rows, beginning and ending with a WS row.

Shape Front Neck
Front neck cast-off row (RS): K26 (27, 28, 29, 32, 33, 35, 38, 38, 39) sts, join new ball of yarn and cast off centre 31 (32, 31, 32, 33, 36, 37, 40, 43, 44) sts for front neck, k to end. *26 (27, 28, 29, 32, 33, 35, 38, 38, 39) sts rem for both left and right fronts*
Working right and left front separately now.

Right Front
Continuing where yarn is attached purl across one WS row.
Neck dec row (RS): K1, ssk, k to end. *1 st dec; 25 (26, 27, 28, 31, 32, 34, 37, 37, 38) sts rem*
Continue in St st and rep neck dec row every RS row a further 6 (7, 7, 8, 9, 9, 10, 11, 10, 11) times. *19 (19, 20, 20, 22, 23, 24, 26, 27, 27) sts rem*

Continue in St st for another 7 (7, 7, 7, 5, 5, 3, 3, 5, 5) rows beginning and ending with a WS row.

Shape Right Front Shoulder
Short row 1 (RS): K to last 7 (7, 7, 7, 8, 8, 8, 9, 9, 9) sts, wrap and turn.
Short row 2 (WS): P to neck edge, turn.
Short row 3: K to 6 (6, 7, 7, 7, 8, 8, 9, 9, 9) sts before prev wrapped st, wrap and turn.
Short row 4: P to neck edge, turn.
Next row (RS): K to end, working wraps together with wrapped sts
Next row (WS): Purl.
Break yarn. Transfer 19 (19, 20, 20, 22, 23, 24, 26, 27, 27) right shoulder sts to waste yarn.

Left Front
Continuing where yarn is attached purl across one WS row.
Neck dec row (RS): K to last 3 sts of row, k2tog, k1. *1 st dec; 25 (26, 27, 28, 31, 32, 34, 37, 37, 38) sts rem*

Continue in St st and rep neck dec row every RS row a further 6 (7, 7, 8, 9, 9, 10, 11, 10, 11) times. *19 (19, 20, 20, 22, 23, 24, 26, 27, 27) sts rem*

Continue in St st for another 8 (8, 8, 8, 6, 6, 4, 4, 6, 6) rows beginning with a WS row and ending with a RS row.

Shape Left Front Shoulder
Short row 1 (WS): P to 7 (7, 7, 7, 8, 8, 8, 9, 9, 9) sts before end of row, wrap and turn.
Short row 2: K to neck edge, turn.
Short row 3: P to 6 (6, 7, 7, 7, 8, 8, 9, 9, 9) sts before prev wrapped st, wrap and turn.
Short row 4: K to neck edge, turn.
Next row (WS): P to end, working wraps together with wrapped sts.
Break yarn. Transfer 19 (19, 20, 20, 22, 23, 24, 26, 27, 27) left shoulder sts to waste yarn.

Join the shoulders with a three-needle cast off as folls:
Turn the knitting to the WS and return the left back shoulder sts to needles. Hold the left front shoulder sts parallel with the left back shoulder sts. Using a third needle and working from the armhole edge to the neck edge knit together the first stitch from the front needle with the first stitch on the rear needle. *Knit together the next stitch from the front and rear needles. Cast off one stitch on the right needle tip as normal. Repeat from * until all stitches have been joined and cast off.
Repeat this process for the right front and back shoulder sts.

SLEEVES
Count 12 (12, 12, 14, 14, 14, 14, 16, 16, 16) rows down from the shoulder seam on each side of the armhole and place a locking marker in the 13th (13th, 13th, 15th, 15th, 15th, 15th, 17th, 17th, 17th) row.

With RS facing, using MC yarn and 3.25mm / US 3 DPNs or long circular needle, and beginning at the shoulder seam, pick up and knit 1 stitch at the shoulder join, PM, pick up and knit 9 (9, 9, 10, 10, 10, 10, 12, 12, 12) sts to marker, 26 (27, 29, 30, 31, 32, 34, 34, 37, 39) sts to bottom of armhole, k7 (9, 10, 11, 12, 13, 14, 15, 16, 17) along underarm sts, PM, k2tog (this will be the centre underarm st), PM, k7 (9, 10, 11, 12, 13, 14, 15, 16, 17) sts along remainder of underarm sts, 26 (27, 29, 30, 31, 32, 34, 34, 37, 39) sts to marker, 9 (9, 9, 10, 10, 10, 10, 12, 12, 12) sts to shoulder seam. Pm for beg of round. *86 (92, 98, 104, 108, 112, 118, 124, 132, 138) sts total (2 seam sts with markers either side at top of shoulder and centre underarm. Locking markers can now be removed).*

Shape Sleeve Cap
Note: *Cap is shaped using the Wrap & Turn method of short rows. Do not pick up wraps for this section.*
Short row 1 (RS): K1 (centre shoulder st), SM, k9 (9, 9, 10, 10, 10, 10, 12, 12, 12), wrap and turn.
Short row 2 (WS): P19 (19, 19, 21, 21, 21, 21, 25, 25, 25) (going past centre shoulder st) wrap and turn.
Short row 3: K to prev wrapped st, k wrapped st, k1, wrap and turn.
Short row 4: P to prev wrapped st, p wrapped st, p1, wrap and turn.
Short rows 5–6: Repeat short rows 3–4 once more.
Short row 7: K to prev wrapped st, k wrapped st, wrap and turn.
Short row 8: P to prev wrapped st, p wrapped st, wrap and turn.
Repeat short rows 7 and 8 a further 14 (14, 16, 17, 18, 19, 21, 21, 24, 26) times, at which point there will be 13 (16, 17, 18, 19, 20, 21, 22, 23, 24) sts rem unworked before the centre underarm marker on each side.

Note: *In the next section you will wrap 2 sts with every turn. Work the same as a single wrap and turn but slip 2 sts together instead of 1.*
Short row 1: K to prev wrapped st, k wrapped st, wrap 2 sts and turn.
Short row 2: P to prev wrapped st, p wrapped st, wrap 2 sts and turn.
Short row 3: K to prev wrapped sts, k2tog, wrap 2 sts and turn. *1 st dec*
Short row 4: P to prev wrapped sts, p2tog, wrap 2 sts and turn. *1 st dec; 84 (90, 96, 102, 106, 110, 116, 122, 130, 136) sts*

Sizes 2–10 only
Short rows 5–6: Repeat short rows 3–4 once more. *2 sts dec; – (88, 94, 100, 104, 108, 114, 120, 128, 134) sts*

All sizes
Note: *The final pair of short rows only wraps a single stitch each time.*
Next short row: K to prev wrapped sts, k2tog, wrap 1 st and turn. *1 st dec*
Next short row: P to prev wrapped sts, p2tog, wrap 1 st and turn. *1 st dec; 82 (86, 92, 98, 102, 106, 112, 118, 126, 132) sts*
Next row (RS): K to beg of round marker.

Shape sleeve
Begin working in the round.
Next round: K to prev wrapped stitch, k2tog, k to 1 st before next wrapped st, k2tog, k to end. *2 sts dec; 80 (84, 90, 96, 100, 104, 110, 116, 124, 130) sts rem*

The beg of the round is now moved to the underside of the arm. You will essentially swap the placement of the BOR marker and second marker (still keeping two markers total in place):
Partial round: Make sure that the beg of round marker at top of shoulder now becomes the second marker, k40 (42, 45, 48, 50, 52, 55, 58, 62, 65), replace beg of round marker at the underarm.
Continue to work St st in the round until sleeve measures 5 (6.5, 7.5, 7.5, 7.5, 7.5, 7.5, 7.5, 7.5, 7.5)cm / 2 (2½, 3, 3, 3, 3, 3, 3, 3, 3)" from underarm.

Inc round: *K1, SM, k2, M1L, k to 2 sts before next marker, M1R, k2, SM; rep from * once more. *4 sts inc*
Knit 7 (7, 8, 7, 8, 9, 8, 11, 19, 29) rounds. Repeat last 8 (8, 9, 8, 9, 10, 9, 12, 20, 30) rounds a further 8 (7, 6, 7, 6, 5, 6, 4, 2, 1) times. *36 (32, 28, 32, 28, 24, 28, 20, 12, 8) sts inc; 116 (116, 118, 128, 128, 128, 138, 136, 136, 138) sts*

Sizes 1, 2, 8 and 9 only
Work inc round once more. *4 sts inc; 120 (120, –, –, –, –, –, 140, 140, –) sts*

Sizes 3, 4, 5, 6, 7 and 10 only
Inc round: *K1, SM, k2, M1L, k to next marker, SM; rep from * once more. *2 sts inc; – (–, 120, 130, 130, 130, 140, –, –, 140) sts*
Second marker can now be removed.

All sizes
Knit 3 (6, 2, 1, 2, 5, 2, 5, 5, 5) rounds. Change to 3.5mm / US 4 DPNs or long circular needle.
Set-up round: Using MC, p to end.
Now work from the Stripe Sequence pattern starting at row 1 with CC1, and work pattern as folls:
Round 1: [Yo, k3, sk2po, k3, yo, k1] 12 (12, 12, 13, 13, 13, 14, 14, 14, 14) times.
Round 2: P to end.
Last 2 rounds set Razor Shell Pattern. Continue in Razor Shell Pattern changing colours as indicated, until Stripe Sequence row 52 is complete.

Change to 3.25mm / US 3 DPNs or long circular needle.
Knit 8 rounds straight using MC. If row tension is correct, sleeve now measures 42.5cm / 16¾" from underarm.
Dec round: [K2tog] to end. *60 (60, 60, 65, 65, 65, 70, 70, 70, 70) sts dec; 60 (60, 60, 65, 65, 65, 70, 70, 70, 70) sts rem*

Sizes 1–6, 9 and 10 only
Dec round: *K13 (13, 13, 11, 11, 63, –, –, 33, 33), k2tog; rep from * to end. *4 (4, 4, 5, 5, 1, –, –, 2, 2) sts dec; 56 (56, 56, 60, 60, 64, –, –, 68, 68) sts rem*

Sizes 7 and 8 only
Next round (dec): K6, *k2tog, k9; rep from * to last 9 sts, k2tog, k7. *6 sts dec; 64 sts rem*

All sizes
Change to 3mm / US 2 DPNs or long circular needle.
Work in 2x2 Rib until cuff measures 10cm / 4".
Cast off all sts in rib.

FINISHING
Neckband
Using 3.25mm / US 3 circular needle, 40cm / 16" length, MC, and starting at the right shoulder join, with RS facing, pick up and knit 45 (48, 47, 50, 53, 56, 59, 64, 65, 68) back neck sts, then pick up and knit 14 (16, 17, 19, 19, 20, 20, 22, 22, 22) sts to front neck sts, pick up and knit 31 (32, 31, 32, 33, 36, 37, 40, 43, 44) cast-off front neck sts, then pick up and knit 14 (16, 17, 19, 19, 20, 20, 22, 22, 22) sts to left shoulder join. *104 (112, 112, 120, 124, 132, 136, 148, 152, 156) sts*
Join for working in the round and PM to indicate beg of round.

Crew neck
Work in 2x2 Rib for 5 rounds then cast off all sts in rib pattern being careful not to cast off too tightly.

Turtleneck
Work in 2x2 Rib until neckband measures 10cm / 4". Change to 3.5mm / US 4 circular needle, 40cm / 16" length and continue in rib pattern for another 11.5cm / 4½". Cast off all sts in rib pattern being careful not to cast off too tightly.

Weave in ends. Block garment to schematic measurements. See Special Techniques for detailed blocking information.

HJARTA SCHEMATIC KEY

a. Hem circumference: 98 (105.5, 113, 120.5, 128, 135.5, 143, 150.5, 158, 165.5)cm / 38½ (41½, 44½, 47½, 50¼, 53¼, 56¼, 59¼, 62¼, 65¼)"

b. Bust circumference: 82 (90.5, 98.5, 107, 115, 123.5, 131.5, 140, 148.5, 156.5)cm / 32¼ (35½, 38¾, 42, 45¼, 48½, 51¾, 55, 58¼, 61¾)"

c. Length to underarm: 67.5cm / 26½"

d. Armhole depth: 19 (19.5, 20.5, 21.5, 22, 22.5, 23.5, 24, 25, 26)cm / 7½ (7¾, 8, 8½, 8¾, 9, 9¼, 9½, 10, 10¼)"

e. Cross shoulder: 31 (32.5, 32.5, 34, 36.5, 38.5, 40.5, 43.5, 45, 46)cm / 12¼ (12¾, 13, 13¼, 14¼, 15, 15¾, 17¼, 17¾, 18)"

f. Neck drop: 5.5 (6, 6, 6.5, 6.5, 6.5, 6.5, 7, 7, 7.5)cm / 2 (2¼, 2¼, 2½, 2½, 2½, 2½, 2¾, 2¾, 3)"

g. Back neck width: 17 (18, 17.5, 19, 20, 21, 22, 24, 24.5, 25.5)cm / 6¾ (7, 7, 7½, 7¾, 8¼, 8¾, 9½, 9¾, 10)"

h. Upper arm circumference: 30 (31.5, 34, 36, 37.5, 39, 41.5, 43.5, 46.5, 49)cm / 11¾ (12½, 13¼, 14¼, 14¾, 15½, 16¼, 17¼, 18¼, 19¼)"

i. Balloon sleeve wrist circumference: 21 (21, 21, 22.5, 22.5, 24, 24, 24, 25.5, 25.5)cm / 8¼ (8¼, 8¼, 9, 9, 9½, 9½, 9½, 10, 10)"

j. Balloon circumference at widest point: 45 (45, 45, 49, 49, 49, 52.5, 52.5, 52.5, 52.5)cm / 17¾ (17¾, 17¾, 19¼, 19¼, 19¼, 20¾, 20¾, 20¾, 20¾)"

k. Balloon sleeve length from underarm: 53cm / 20¾"

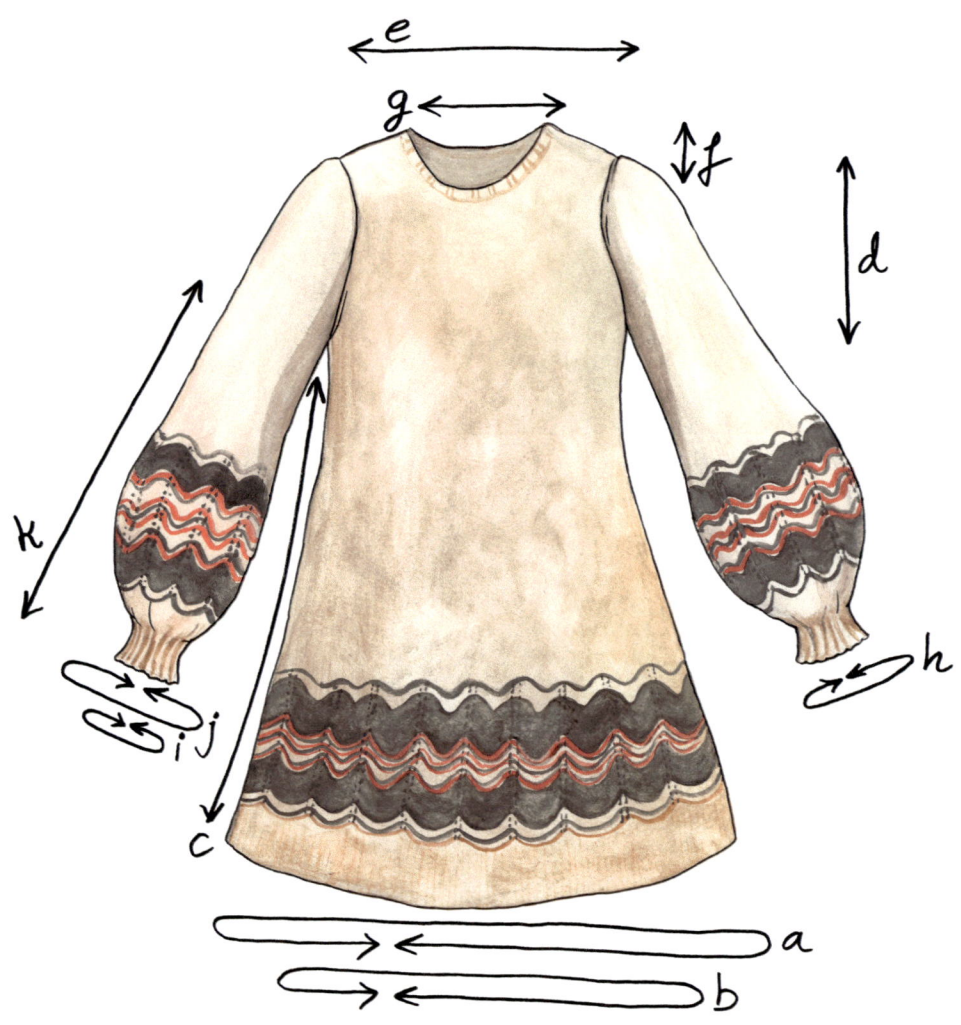

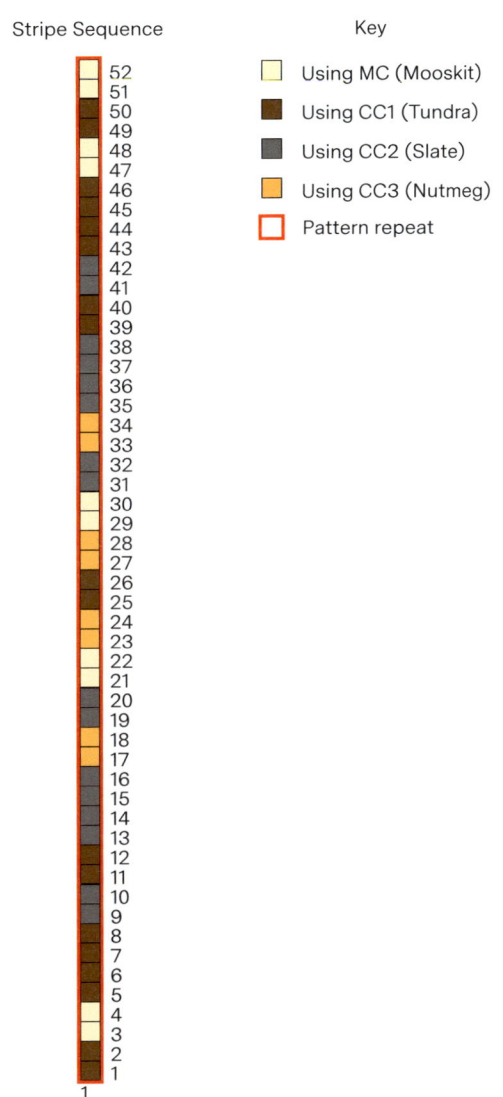

Vatna

Vatna: *'lake' in Shetland dialect.*

Vatna and Tarra are companion shawls using the Razor Shell Lace pattern. Vatna is the larger version. My mum included haps (traditional Shetland shawls) as part of her offerings in her made-to-order knitwear business but, as I already have a hap pattern in existence, I decided to do a slightly different version here.

Typically, Old Shell Lace is used for haps in Shetland but as Razor Shell Lace (or New Shell Lace) appears so much in this book, I thought it would be nice to insert it in this hap-esque accessory. As with traditional haps, this is worked on a garter stitch background and you can have endless fun choosing your colour combinations!

One Size:
Wingspan: Approx 134cm / 52¾"
Depth: 67cm / 26½"

Yarn (fingering / 4-ply-weight yarn in the following amounts):

Jamieson & Smith 2ply Jumper Weight (fingering / 4-ply-weight; 100% Real Shetland Wool; 115m / 125yds per 25g ball)
MC: Shade 32; 5 balls
CC1: Shade 54; 2 balls
CC2: Shade FC61; 1 ball
CC3: Shade 125; 1 ball
OR approx
MC: 570m / 620yds
CC1: 155m / 165yds
CC2: 105m / 110yds
CC3: 75m / 80yds

Gauge:
19 sts & 26 rows = 10cm / 4" over Razor Shell Pattern on 4.5mm needles after blocking

19 sts & 24 rows = 10cm / 4" over Garter Stitch on 4.5mm needles after blocking

Needles:
4.5mm / US 7 circular needle, 60cm / 24" and 100cm / 40" length

5.5mm / US 9 circular needle, 100cm / 40" length (for the cast on)

Always use a needle size that will result in the correct gauge after blocking.

Notions:
3 stitch markers, 1 locking stitch marker (optional), tapestry needle for weaving in ends

Notes:
The shawl is worked from the outside in, starting with the widest edge. The body of the shawl is shaped by decreases that are evenly distributed across the main fabric until only a few stitches remain.

Stitch Glossary:
Stripe Sequence
Also shown on chart.
Rows 1–2: MC
Rows 3–4: CC1
Rows 5–6: MC
Rows 7–10: CC1
Rows 11–12: MC
Rows 13–14: CC1
Rows 15–18: CC2
Rows 19–20: CC3
Rows 21–22: CC2
Rows 23–24: MC
Rows 25–26: CC3
Rows 27–28: CC1
Rows 29–30: CC3
Rows 31–32: MC
Rows 33–34: CC2
Rows 35–36: CC3
Rows 37–40: CC2
Rows 41–42: CC1
Rows 43–44: MC
Rows 45–48: CC1
Rows 49–50: MC
Rows 51–52: CC1
Rows 53–56: MC

PATTERN BEGINS

Razor Shell Border
Note: *Use Splicing for changing colours during Stripe Sequence (see Special Techniques). If desired, add a locking stitch marker on the right side of the fabric once a few rows have been worked.*
Using 5.5mm / US 9 circular needle, 100cm / 40" length, MC, and the long-tail method, cast on 381 sts.
Change to 4.5mm / US 7 circular needle, 100cm / 40" length and knit 1 row.

Following the Stripe Sequence, starting at row 1, work as folls:
Row 1 (RS): K2, [yo, k5, sk2po, k5, yo, k1] rep to last st, k1.
Row 2 (WS): Knit.
Rep rows 1 and 2 a further 12 times (26 rows of Razor Shell worked).

Row 27 (RS, dec): K2, [yo, k4, sl2 kwise, k3tog, psso, k4, yo, k1] rep to last st, k1. *54 sts dec; 327 sts rem*
Row 28 (WS): Knit.
Row 29: K2, [yo, k4, sk2po, k4, yo, k1] rep to last st, k1.
Row 30: Knit.
Rep rows 29 and 30 a further 12 times.

Row 55 (RS, dec): K2, [yo, k3, sl2 kwise, k3tog, psso, k3, yo, k1] rep to last st, k1. *54 sts dec; 273 sts rem*
Row 56 (WS): Knit.

Upper Body of Shawl
Note: *In the following set-up row it may appear as if the markers are placed unequally. If you work as written, they will in fact be correct, and will ensure that the decreases line up.*
Set-up row (RS): K2, yo, ssk, k64, PM, k70, PM, k70, PM, k to last 4 sts, k2tog, yo, k2.
Next row (WS): Knit.
Row 1 (RS, dec): K2, yo, sssk, *k to 3 sts before marker, sk2po, remove marker, k1, replace marker; rep from * twice more, k to last 5 sts, k3tog, yo, k2. *8 sts dec*
Row 2 (WS): Knit.
Row 3: K2, yo, ssk, k to last 4 sts, k2tog, yo, k2.
Row 4: Knit.
Rep rows 1–4 a further 15 times. *128 sts dec; 145 sts rem*

Row 65 (RS, dec): K2, yo, sssk, *k to 3 sts before marker, sk2po, remove marker, k1, replace marker; rep from * twice more, k to last 5 sts, k3tog, yo, k2. *8 sts dec*
Row 66: Knit.
Rep rows 65–66 a further 13 times. *112 sts dec; 33 sts rem*

Row 93 (RS, dec): K2, yo, sssk, sk2po, remove marker, *k7, sk2po, remove marker; rep from * once more, k3tog, yo, k2. *8 sts dec; 25 sts rem*
Row 94: Knit.
Row 95 (RS, dec): K2, yo, sssk, k5, sl2 kwise, k3tog, psso, k5, k3tog, yo, k2. *6 sts dec; 19 sts rem*
Row 96: Knit.
Row 97 (dec): K2, yo, sssk, k2, sl2 kwise, k3tog, psso, k2, k3tog, yo, k2. *6 sts dec; 13 sts rem*
Row 98: Knit.
Row 99 (dec): K2, yo, sssk, sk2po, k3tog, yo, k2. *4 sts dec; 9 sts rem*
Row 100: Knit.
Row 101 (dec): K2, sl2 kwise, k3tog, psso, k2. *4 sts dec; 5 sts rem*
Row 102: Knit.
Row 103 (dec): Sl2 kwise, k3tog, psso. *4 sts dec; 1 st rem*
Break yarn and draw through remaining stitch.

FINISHING
Weave in ends. Block shawl firmly to schematic measurements, pinning out the points of the Razor Shell border. See Special Techniques for more blocking information.

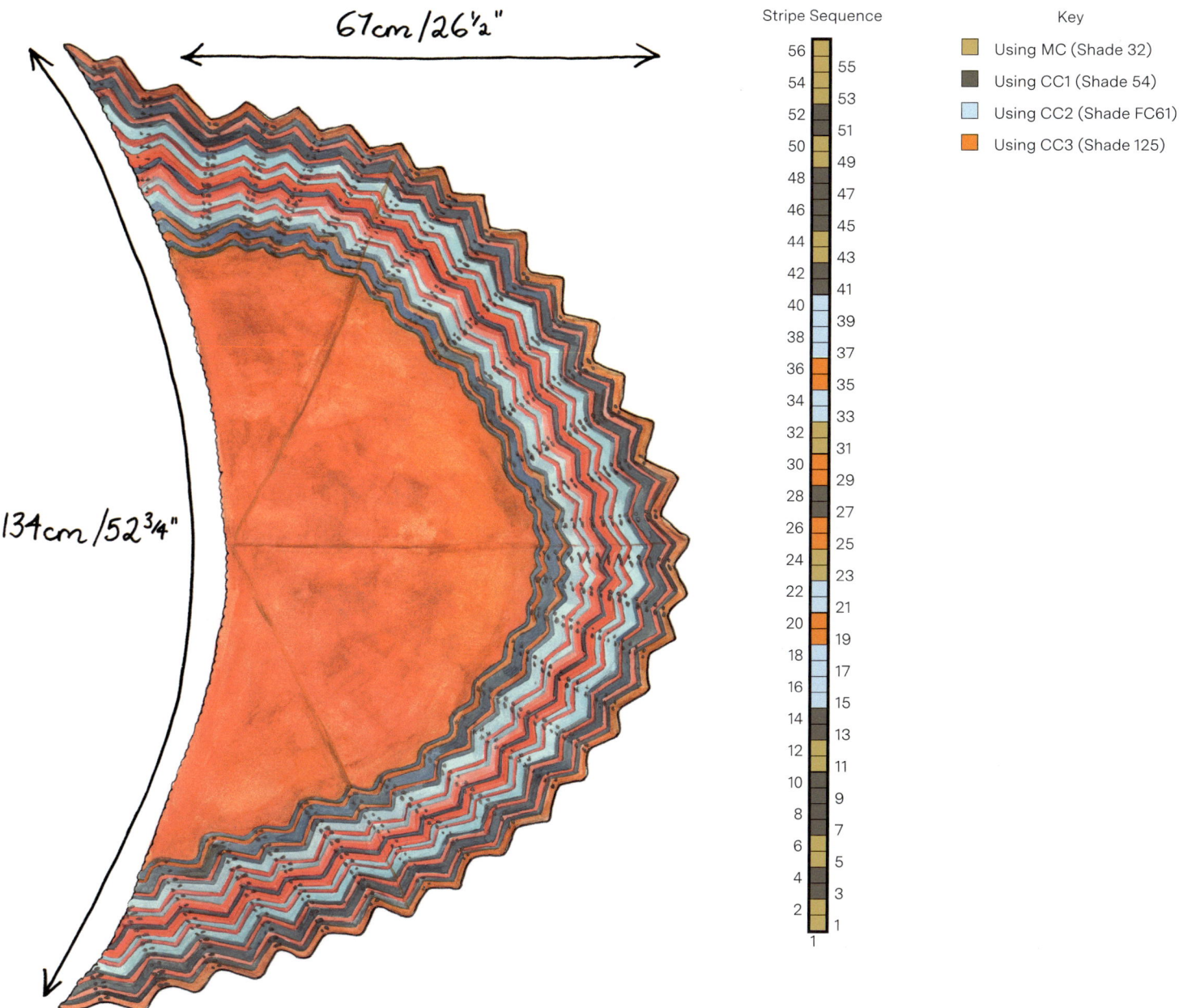

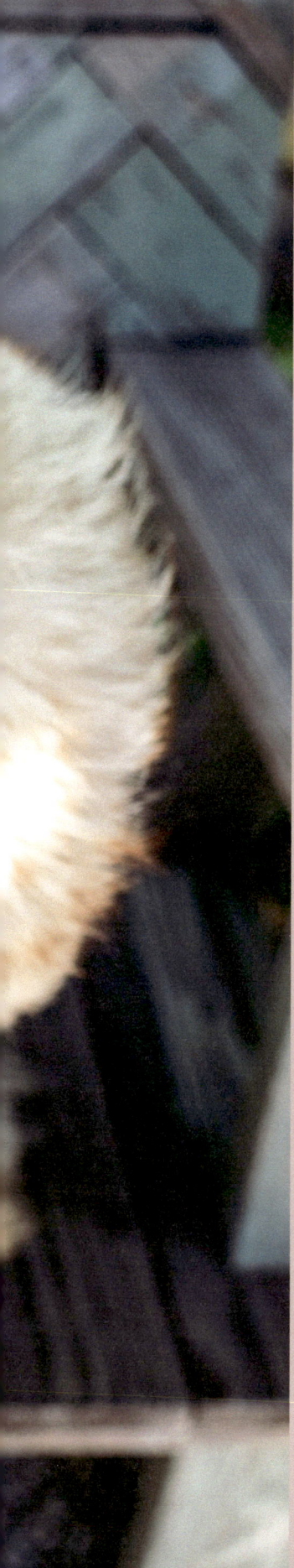

Smora

Smora: *'clover' in Shetland dialect.*

Mum sold dozens of different hat designs in her little shop on Burns Lane, Lerwick. These hats are not a specific replication of any single hat, but a combination of several.

I love a good deep-brimmed beanie that will protect my ears from the elements but when you are feeling a little jaunty (and when the weather is calmer), it's nice to have a beret option to reach for!

One Size (Two variations):

Beret (Beanie)
Circumference at brim: 46.5cm / 18¼" for both versions
Length from brim to crown as worn: 23 (24) cm / 9 (9½)"
Circumference at widest point: 72 (54) cm / 28½ (21¼)"

Yarn (fingering / 4-ply-weight yarn in the following amounts):

Colourway 1
Beret shown in:
Jamieson & Smith 2ply Jumper Weight (fingering / 4-ply-weight; 100% Real Shetland Wool; 115m / 125yds per 25g ball)
MC: Shade 81; 2 balls (will need additional ball if adding Pom Pom)
CC1: Shade FC43; 1 ball
CC2: Shade 3; 1 ball
CC3: Shade 4; 1 ball
CC4: Shade 1281; 1 ball
OR approx
MC: 165m / 180yds
CC1: 37m / 40yds
CC2: 32m / 35yds
CC3: 14m / 15yds
CC4: 14m / 15yds

Colourway 2
Beanie shown in:
Jamieson's of Shetland Spindrift (fingering / 4-ply-weight; 100% Shetland Wool; 105m / 115yds per 25g ball)
MC: Camel; 2 balls (will need additional ball if adding Pom Pom)
CC1: Auld Gold; 1 ball
CC2: Moorit; 1 ball
CC3: Eesit; 1 ball
CC4: Cocoa; 1 ball
OR approx
MC: 185m / 200yds
CC1: 27.5m / 30yds
CC2: 18m / 20yds
CC3: 9m / 10yds
CC4: 9m / 10yds

Gauge:
27 sts & 32 rounds = 10cm / 4" over Fair Isle Pattern on 3.5mm needles after blocking

28 sts & 40 rounds = 10cm / 4" in Rib Pattern on 3mm needles after blocking

Needles:
3.5mm / US 4 circular needle, 40cm / 16" length (for body of hat)

3.5mm / US 4 DPNs or long circular needle (if working magic loop for crown of hat)

3mm / US 2 circular needle, 40cm / 16" length (for brim)

Always use a needle size that will result in the correct gauge after blocking.

Notions:
1 stitch marker, tapestry needle for weaving in ends

Notes:
Where instructions differ for beret and beanie, instructions for beret will appear first with instructions for beanie in parentheses.

Stitch Glossary:
2x2 Rib (in the round):
Round 1: [K2, p2] to end.
Rep round 1 for pattern.

Abbreviations:
K1-r/b: Knit 1 into row below; Turn the LH needle slightly towards you so that the WS of the work can be seen. Insert RH needle form the top down into the purl stitch that sits below the first st on the LH needle. Knit this stitch then knit the stitch on the needle.

A full list of abbreviations appears on page 145.

PATTERN BEGINS

BRIM
Using 3mm / US 2 circular needle, 40cm / 16" length and MC, cast on 128 sts as folls:
Make a slipknot and place on needle as the first cast-on stitch.
Cast on 1 st using the long-tail method, then cast on 2 sts using the German twisted method (see Special Techniques), *cast on 2 sts using the long-tail method, then cast on 2 sts using the German twisted method; rep from * until 128 sts have been cast on.

Join for working in the round being careful not to twist. PM to indicate beg of round. Work in 2x2 Rib for 16 (44) rounds. If row tension is correct, piece will measure 4 (11) cm / 1½ (4½)".

Beret Only
Inc round: *[K1-r/b] twice, p2; rep from * to end. *64 sts inc; 192 sts*

Beanie Only
Inc round: *K1-r/b, k1, p2, k2, p2; rep from * to end. *16 sts inc; 144 sts*

Both Versions
Change to 3.5mm / US 4 circular needle, 40cm / 16" length and knit 1 round in MC.

Begin Fair Isle Chart as folls:
Round 1: Work across 12 sts from row 1 of Chart A 16 (12) times.
Last round sets chart pattern. Continue to work from chart, changing yarns as indicated, until chart row 32 is complete.

Note: *During the crown shaping chart 16 (12) sts are decreased every decrease round. It is necessary to stop 1 before the beginning of each decrease round and then slip this last to right needle, remove marker, return slipped to left needle, replace marker and then begin decrease round.*
Begin Crown Shaping chart as folls:
Round 1: Work across 24 sts from row 1 of Crown Shaping Chart 8 (6) times.
Last round sets chart pattern. Continue to work from chart, changing yarns and decreasing as indicated (see note above), until chart row 24 is complete. *176 (132) sts dec; 16 (12) sts rem*

Beret Only: [K2tog] to end. *8 sts dec; 8 sts rem*

Both Versions
Cut yarn and draw through remaining sts.

FINISHING
Weave in ends. Block to measurements. See Special Techniques for more blocking information.

Add pom pom (optional).

SMORA SCHEMATIC KEY

Beret (Beanie)

a. **Circumference at brim:**
46.5cm / 18¼" for both versions

b. **Length from brim to crown as worn:**
23 (24) cm / 9 (9½)"

c. **Circumference at widest point:**
72 (54) cm / 28½ (21¼)"

Chart A

Chart B: Crown Shaping
(see written instructions for decrease rounds)

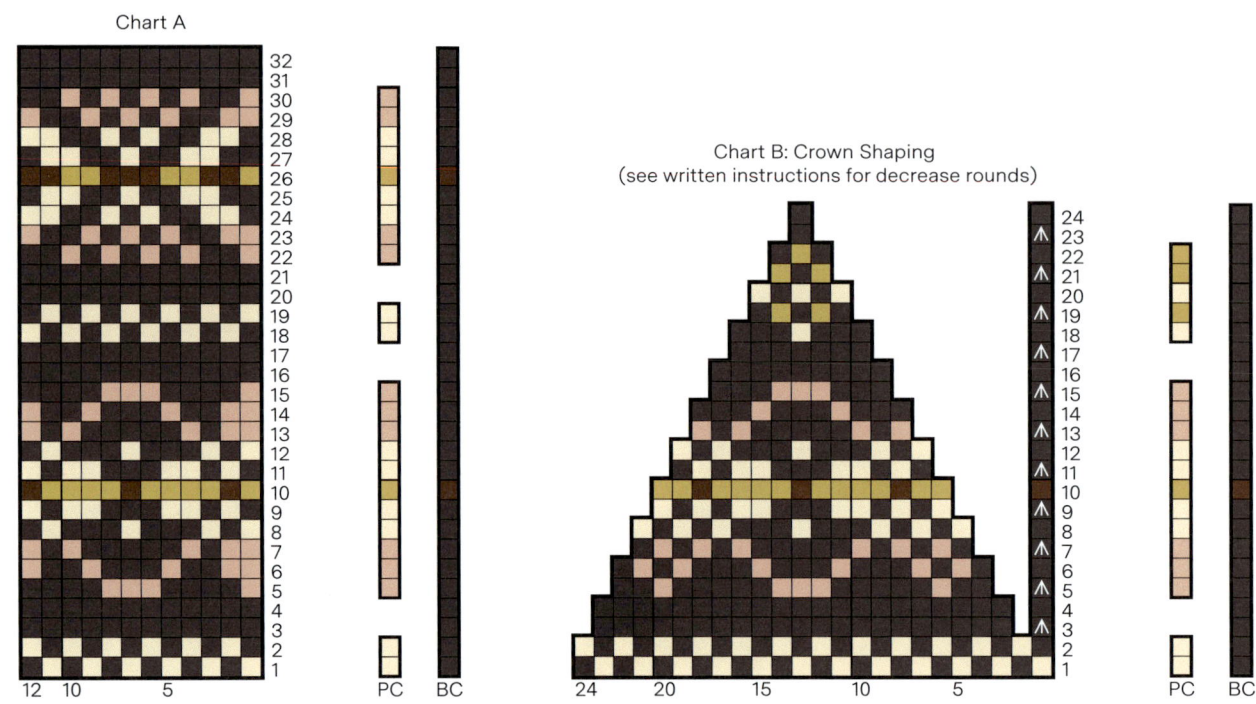

Jamieson & Smith
Colourway 1

- Using MC (Shade 81); knit
- Using CC1 (Shade FC43); knit
- Using CC2 (Shade 3); knit
- Using CC3 (Shade 4); knit
- Using CC4 (Shade 1281); knit
- Using shade indicated; sl2 as if to k2tog, k1, p2sso
- PC Pattern colour
- BC Background colour

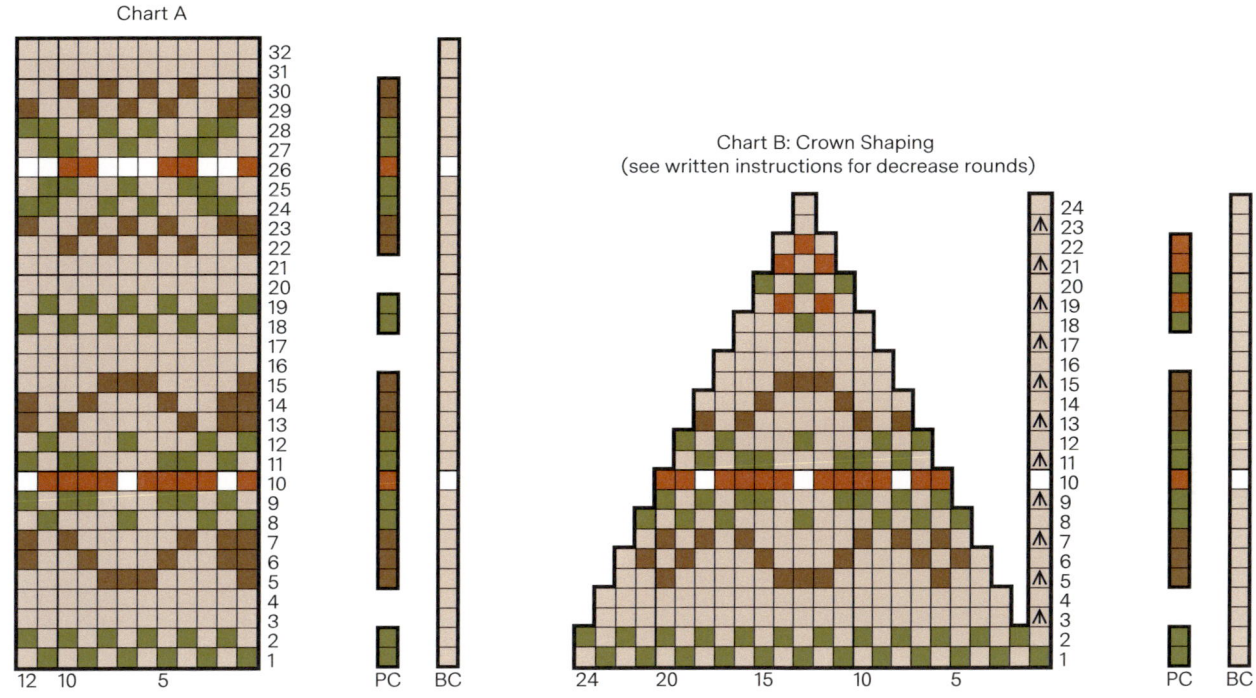

Jamieson's of Shetland
Colourway 2

- Using MC (Camel); knit
- Using CC1 (Auld Gold); knit
- Using CC2 (Moorit); knit
- Using CC3 (Eesit); knit
- Using CC4 (Cocoa); knit
- ⋀ Using shade indicated; sl2 as if to k2tog, k1, p2sso
- PC Pattern colour
- BC Background colour

Snaraness

Snaraness: *another home we briefly lived in while my dad was renovating the ruined croft, Little Bousta.*

There are multiple photos of Mum in a knitted lace headscarf during her time running The Shetland Trader, so I knew early on that I wanted to include one in this collection. This is the only item in the book shown in laceweight.

Of course, if you prefer a slightly warmer and thicker texture, you could easily knit this in a heavier weight instead. This head covering can easily be made larger by working more repeats of the lace chart.

One Size:
Wingspan: Approx 70.5cm / 27¾"
Depth: 35.5cm / 14"

Yarn (laceweight yarn in the following amounts):

169m / 185yds yards of laceweight yarn.

Shown in:
Jamieson & Smith 2ply Lace Weight (laceweight; 50% Real Shetland Wool, 50% Lambswool; 169m / 185yds per 25g ball)
Yellow version:
Shade: L28; 1 ball

Orange version:
Shade: L125; 1 ball

Gauge:
17 sts & 33 rows = 10cm / 4" over Lace Pattern on 4mm needles after blocking

Needles:
4.5mm / US 6 circular needle, 60cm / 24" length

Always use a needle size that will result in the correct gauge after blocking.

Notions:
Stitch markers to separate out lace repeats (optional), 1 locking stitch marker to mark odd numbered rows (optional), tapestry needle for weaving in ends

Notes:
This shawl begins at the point of the triangle and is shaped by making yarn overs at the beginning of every row, increasing the stitch count by 1 st every row. It is easy to make this triangle larger or smaller by adjusting the number of times the repeated section is worked. As there isn't technically right or wrong side to the work a locking stitch marker can be placed on the odd numbered rows side to help keep track when working the chart.

PATTERN BEGINS

Using 4.5mm / US 6 circular needle, 60cm / 24" length, make a slipknot and place onto the needle as the first stitch.
Set-up row: Kfb into the stitch on the needle. *1 st inc, 2 sts on needle*

Note: *Please see Special Techniques for how to work a yarn over at the beginning of the row*

Charted Instructions
See below for written instructions.
Row 1 (RS): Reading from right to left, work across row 1 of Chart A. *1 st inc*
Row 2 (WS): Reading from left to right, work across row 2 of Chart A. *1 st inc*
Last 2 rows set Chart A pattern. Work as set until Chart A is complete. *20 sts inc; 22 sts*

Note: *In the following section, if you wish to use stitch markers for each pattern repeat, it is recommended that you place markers at the start of each marked section in row 1 of Chart B, and remove them on row 8 each time.*
Row 21 (RS): Reading from right to left, work across row 1 of Chart B, working marked section once. *1 st inc*
Row 22 (WS): Reading from left to right, work across row 2 of Chart B, working marked section once. *1 st inc*
Last 2 rows set Chart B pattern. Work as set until Chart B is complete. *8 sts inc; 30 sts*

Row 29 (RS): Reading from right to left, work across row 1 of Chart B, working marked section twice. *1 st inc*
Row 30 (WS): Reading from left to right, work across row 2 of Chart B, working marked section twice. *1 st inc*
Last 2 rows set Chart B pattern. Work as set until Chart B is complete. *8 sts inc; 38 sts*
Continue to work from Chart B, working an extra repeat of the marked section each time, until you have worked Chart B 12 times in total and you have 118 sts. *80 sts inc; 118 sts*
Cast off all sts using the Icelandic Cast-Off (see Special Techniques) or other stretchy cast off of your choice.
Move to finishing instructions below.

Written Instructions
See above for charted instructions.
Row 1 (RS): Yo, k2. *1 st inc; 3 sts*
Row 2 (WS): Yo, k2, k1 tbl. *1 st inc; 4 sts*
Row 3: Yo, k3, k1 tbl. *1 st inc; 5 sts*
Row 4 and all foll even-numbered rows: Yo, k to last st, k1 tbl. *1 st inc*
Row 5: Yo, k2, yo, ssk, k1, k1 tbl. *1 st inc; 7 sts*
Row 7: Yo, k1, k2tog, yo, k1, yo, ssk, k1, k1 tbl. *1 st inc; 9 sts*
Row 9: Yo, k1, k2tog, yo, k3, yo, ssk, k1, k1 tbl. *1 st inc; 11 sts*
Row 11: Yo, k4, yo, sk2po, yo, k4, k1 tbl. *1 st inc; 13 sts*
Row 13: Yo, k2, yo, ssk, k6, yo, ssk, k1, k1 tbl. *1 st inc; 15 sts*
Row 15: Yo, k1, k2tog, yo, k1, yo, ssk, k3, k2tog, yo, k1, yo, ssk, k1, k1 tbl. *1 st inc; 17 sts*
Row 17: Yo, k1, k2tog, yo, k3, yo, ssk, k1, k2tog, yo, k3, yo, ssk, k1, k1 tbl. *1 st inc; 19 sts*
Row 19: Yo, k4, yo, sk2po, yo, k5, yo, sk2po, yo, k4, k1 tbl. *1 st inc; 21 sts*
Row 20 (WS): As row 4. *1 st inc; 22 sts*
Row 21 (RS): Yo, k2, yo, ssk, k3, [PM, k3, yo, ssk, k3] to last 7 sts, k3, yo, ssk, k1, k1 tbl. *1 st inc*
Row 22 and all foll even-numbered rows: Yo, k to last st (slipping markers), k1 tbl. *1 st inc*
Row 23: Yo, k1, k2tog, yo, k1, yo, ssk, k2, [SM, k1, k2tog, yo, k1, yo, ssk, k2] to last 8 sts, k1, k2tog, yo, k1, yo, ssk, k1, k1 tbl. *1 st inc*
Row 25: Yo, k1, k2tog, yo, k3, yo, ssk, k1, [SM, k2tog, yo, k3, yo, ssk, k1] to last 9 sts, k2tog, yo, k3, yo, ssk, k1, k1 tbl. *1 st inc*
Row 27: Yo, k4, yo, sk2po, yo, k3, [SM, k2, yo, sk2po, yo, k3] to last 10 sts, k2, yo, sk2po, yo, k4, k1 tbl. *1 st inc*
Row 28 (WS): As row 22, but remove all markers. *1 st inc*
Rep rows 21–28 a further 11 times, replacing markers in row 21 each time. Each rep of these 8 rows adds 8 sts. *96 sts inc; 118 sts*

Cast off all sts using the Icelandic Cast-Off (see Special Techniques) or other stretchy cast off of your choice.

FINISHING
Weave in ends. Block shawl firmly to schematic measurements. Catch and pin out each yarn over stitch from the two sides of the triangle to create a decorative effect. See Special Techniques for more blocking information.

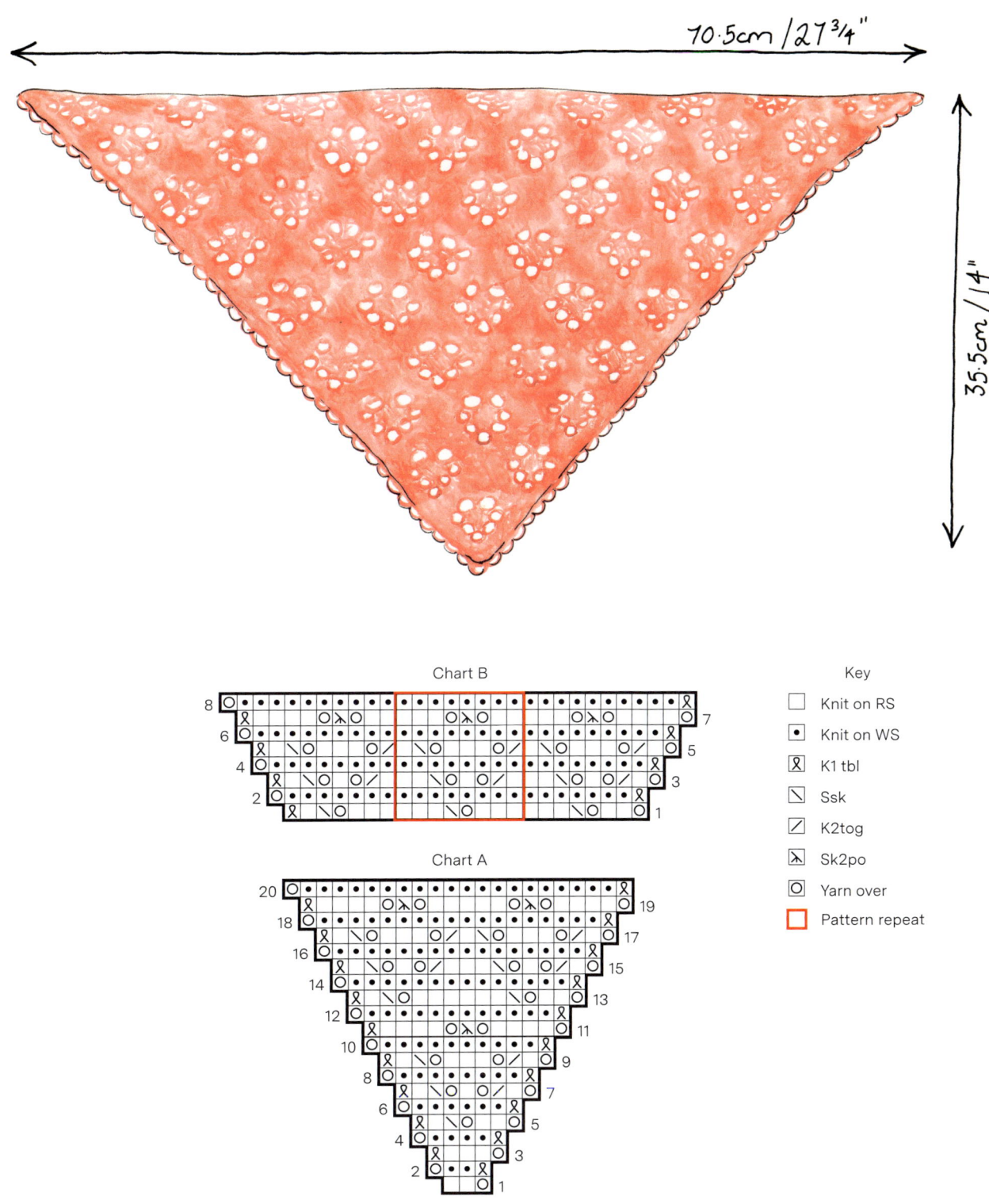

Tarra

Tarra: *'little hill' in Shetland dialect.*

This is the smaller, more scarf-like interpretation of Vatna. It uses the same Razor Shell Lace patterning but has a shallower body that is shaped with the use of short rows.

One Size:

Wingspan: Approx 140.5cm / 55 ¼"
Depth: 30cm / 11¾"

Yarn (fingering / 4-ply-weight yarn in the following amounts):

Jamieson's of Shetland Spindrift (fingering / 4-ply-weight; 100% Shetland Wool; 105m / 115yds per 25g ball)
MC: Shaela; 2 balls
CC1: Auld Gold; 1 ball
CC2: Camel; 1 ball
CC3: Cocoa; 1 ball
OR approx
MC: 145m / 155yds
CC1: 120m / 130yds
CC2: 105m / 110yds
CC3: 35m / 35yds

Gauge:
18 sts & 26 rows = 10cm / 4" over Razor Shell Pattern on 4.5mm needles after blocking

17 sts & 24 rows = 10cm / 4" over Garter Stitch on 4.5mm needles after blocking

Needles:
4.5mm / US 7 circular needle, 100cm / 40" length

5.5mm / US 9 circular needle, 100cm / 40" length (for the cast on)

Always use a needle size that will result in the correct gauge after blocking.

Notions:
Tapestry needle for weaving in ends

Notes:
The shawl is worked from the outside in, starting with the widest edge. The body of the shawl is worked with a combination of short rows and some decreasing, creating a shallow shape and resulting in a long cast-off section at the end.

Stitch Glossary:
Stripe Sequence
Also shown on chart.
Rows 1–2: CC1
Rows 3–4: CC2
Rows 5–6: CC1
Rows 7–10: CC2
Rows 11–12: CC1
Rows 13–14: CC3
Rows 15–16: MC
Rows 17–18: CC3
Rows 19–20: CC1
Rows 21–24: CC2
Rows 25–26: CC1
Rows 27–28: CC2
Rows 29–32: CC1

Abbreviations:
wrap and turn: See Special Techniques on page 143.

A full list of abbreviations appears on page 145.

PATTERN BEGINS

Razor Shell Border
Note: *Use Splicing for changing colours during Stripe Sequence (see Special Techniques). If desired, add a locking stitch marker on the right side of the fabric once a few rows have been worked.*
Using 5.5mm / US 9 circular needle, 100cm / 40" length, CC1, and the long-tail method, cast on 381 sts.

Change to 4.5mm / US 7 circular needle, 100cm / 40" length and knit 1 row.

Following the Stripe Sequence, starting at row 1, work as folls:
Row 1 (RS): K2, [yo, k5, sk2po, k5, yo, k1] rep to last st, k1.
Row 2 (WS): Knit.
Rep rows 1 and 2 a further 6 times (14 rows of Razor Shell Pattern worked).
Row 15 (RS, dec): K2, [yo, k4, sl2 kwise, k3tog, psso, k4, yo, k1] rep to last st, k1. *54 sts dec; 327 sts rem*
Row 16 (WS): Knit.
Row 17: K2, [yo, k4, sk2po, k4, yo, k1] rep to last st, k1.
Row 18: Knit.
Rep rows 17 and 18 a further 6 times.

Row 31 (RS, dec): K2, [yo, k3, sl2 kwise, k3tog, psso, k3, yo, k1] rep to last st, k1. *54 sts dec; 273 sts rem*
Row 32 (WS): Knit.

Upper Body of Shawl
Note: *This section is shaped using the Wrap and Turn method of short rows. You will wrap 2 sts with every turn. Work in the same way as a single wrap and turn but slip 2 sts together instead of 1. Do not pick up wraps.*
Change to MC and knit 2 rows.
Short row 1 (RS): K143, wrap 2 sts and turn.
Short row 2 (WS): K13, wrap 2 sts and turn.
Short row 3: Knit to previous wrapped sts, k together the 2 wrapped sts, k6, wrap 2 sts and turn. *1 st dec*
Short row 4: Knit to previous wrapped sts, k together the 2 wrapped sts, k6, wrap 2 sts and turn. *1 st dec*
Rep short rows 3 and 4 a further 6 times. *14 sts dec; 259 sts rem*

Short row 17 (RS): Knit to previous wrapped sts, k together the 2 wrapped sts, k4, wrap 2 sts and turn. *1 st dec*
Short row 18 (WS): Knit to previous wrapped sts, k together the 2 wrapped sts, k4, wrap 2 sts and turn. *1 st dec*
Rep short rows 17 and 18 a further 10 times. *22 sts dec; 237 sts rem*

Short row 39 (RS): Knit to previous wrapped sts, k together the 2 wrapped sts, k4, wrap the last 2 sts and turn. *1 st dec; 236 sts rem*
Short row 40 (WS): Knit to previous wrapped sts k together the 2 wrapped sts, k4, wrap the last 2 sts and turn. *1 st dec; 235 sts rem*
Cast-off row (RS): With 2 sts on the RH needle, knit 1 st from the LH needle then pull the two wrapped sts over this stitch to cast off. Slip stitch on RH needle to LH needle and begin Icelandic Cast-Off (see Special Techniques) until 3 sts remain (2 of these remaining sts are the wrapped sts from the end of Short row 39). With 1 st on the RH needle, k2tog (the remaining wrapped sts) and pull final cast-off st over. Break yarn and draw through remaining stitch.

FINISHING
Weave in ends. Block shawl firmly to schematic measurements, pinning out the points of the Razor Shell border. See Special Techniques for more blocking information.

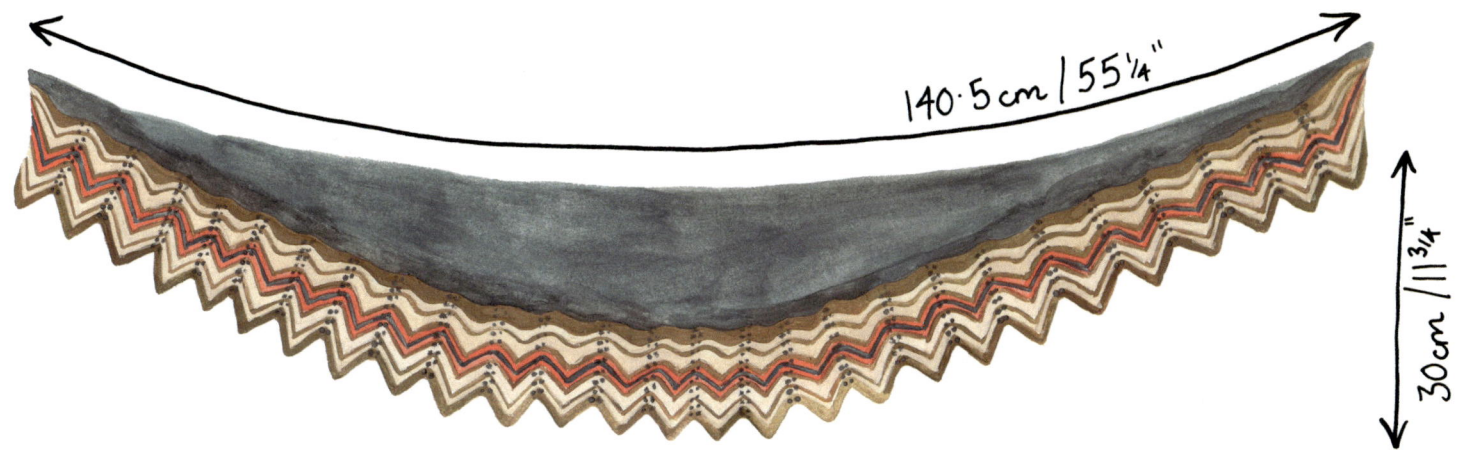

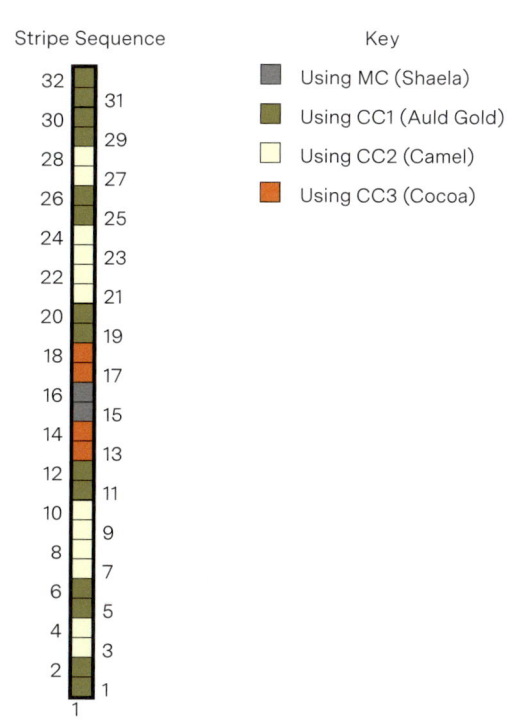

Stripe Sequence

Key

■ Using MC (Shaela)
■ Using CC1 (Auld Gold)
□ Using CC2 (Camel)
■ Using CC3 (Cocoa)

The Shetland Trader / Book Three / Heritage

Special Techniques

Yarn Over at Beginning of Row

Note: This tutorial only shows how the yarn overs are worked at the beginning of each row. Please follow written instructions for pattern.

Hold the working yarn over the RH needle while you work the first stitch from the LH needle.

Note: The working yarn simply sits over the needle. Do not wrap it around the RH needle. You will make these yarn overs at the beginning of every row. Loose loops will form at the outside edges of the work.

You can find a video tutorial here:
youtu.be/REiySOzmW3s

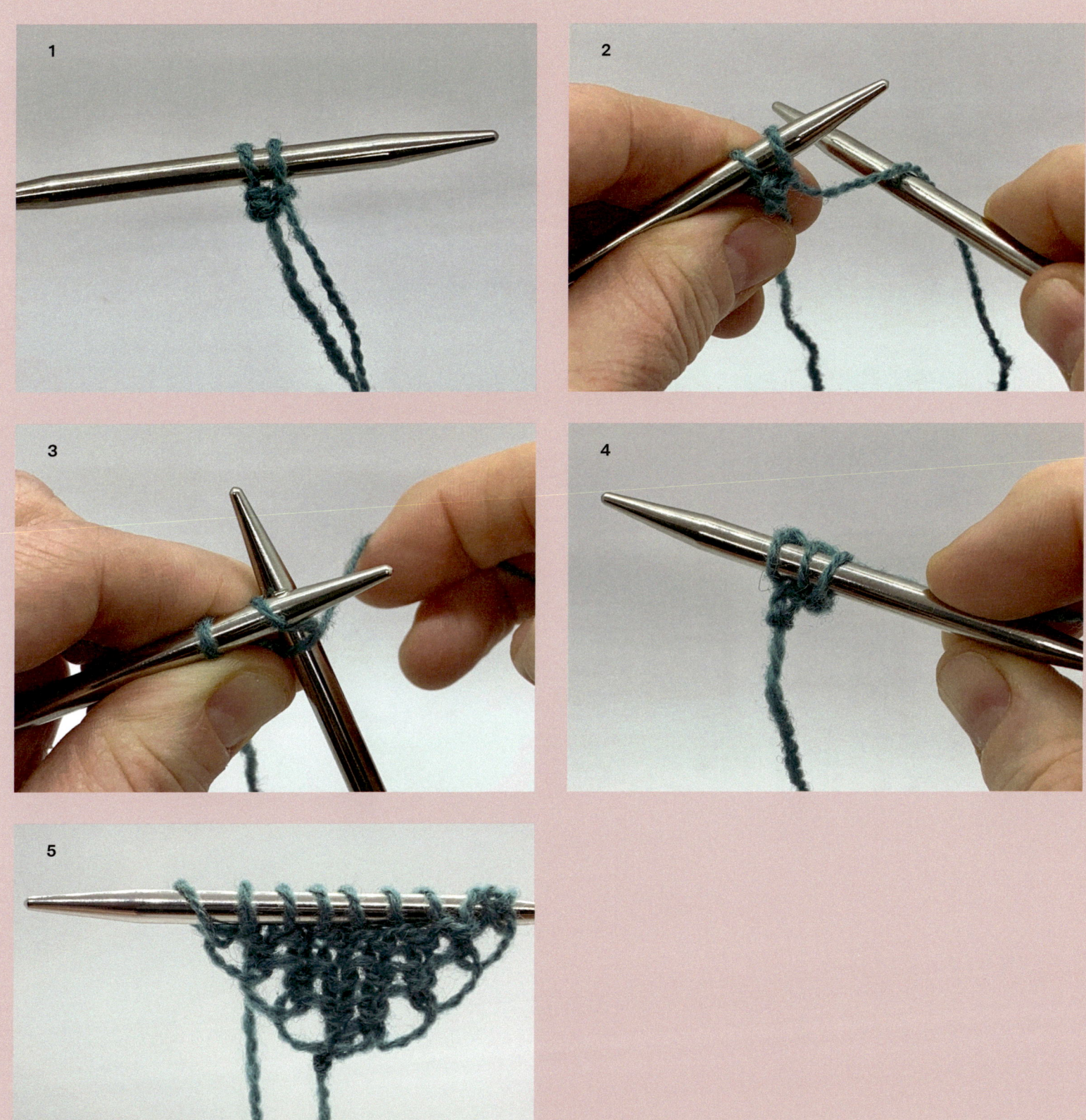

Splicing Yarns

Same method applies to splicing a single colour, although you won't need to do the set-up section.

Set-up section: This may take a little trial and error; it is not an exact science!

To change colour on a particular stitch, work to 10 stitches before the colour change is required. Wrap the working yarn around the needle 10 times and pinch the yarn at this point. Don't wrap too tightly. Let the wraps unravel. Add an extra 5cm / 2" to the working yarn after your pinch, and break the yarn at that point.

Splicing:
Separate the plies for approx 3.75cm / 1½" on both yarns (old and new). Then trim away half of the plies to thin it out a little. Wrap the two yarns around each other at the point at which you trimmed the plies so that the ends of colour go back on themselves. Lay in palm of hand, add moisture (water or saliva) to the join and rub the palms of your hands together vigorously to felt the join until no ends show. You may have to add more moisture or move the work slightly.

You can find a video tutorial here:
youtu.be/QxBD2gSmUjM

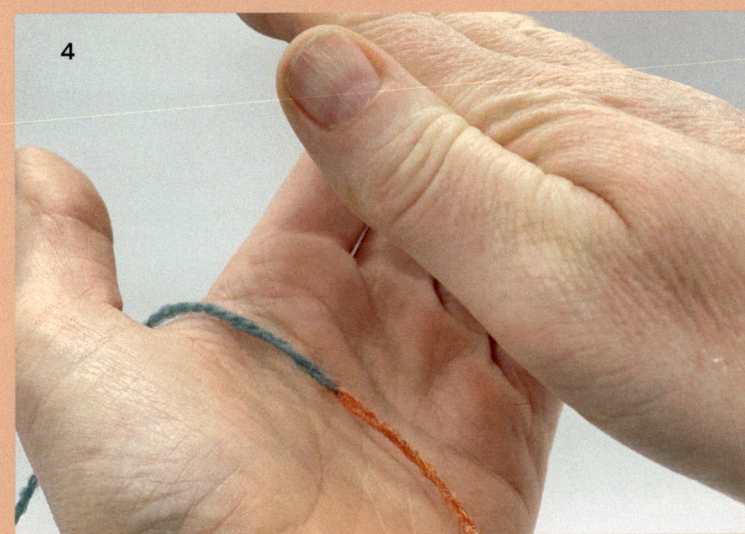

The Shetland Trader / Book Three / Heritage 141

Backwards-Loop Cast-On Method

Step 1: Hold the working yarn over your left thumb so that the yarn attached to the work is at the rear, and the yarn attached to the ball (the tail) is at the front.

Step 2: Grasp the tail of the yarn with your ring and little fingers of the same hand.

Step 3: Bring your right needle tip towards you, so that the yarn attached to the work crosses over the tail.

Step 4: Bring the right needle tip up, parallel with your thumb, into the backwards loop of yarn that has been formed on your thumb.

Step 5: Drop the loop off your thumb and onto the needle tip.

Step 6: Tighten the loop on your needle.

Repeat steps 1–6 until sufficient stitches have been cast on.

Cable Cast-On Method

Step 1: Insert RH needle between the first two stitches on the LH needle.

Step 2: Wrap yarn around RH needle and pull through a loop as you would for a normal knit stitch but do not remove from the LH needle.

Step 3: Being careful not to twist the loop, place it onto LH needle for 1 stitch cast on.

Repeat steps 1-3 for desired number of stitches. Make sure not to work too tightly for this cast-on.

German Twisted Cast-On Method

The set up for this cast-on is the same as for the Long-Tail Cast-On Method. Make a slipknot and place onto the right hand needle. Put the thumb and index finger of your left hand in between the yarns hanging goes around the index finger and the tail end around the thumb. Turn your left hand so that the palm faces up making a V-shape with the yarns. Keep the hanging ends of the yarn in place with your other fingers.

Step 1: Bring needle under both yarns that are around thumb.

Step 2: Bring needle down through the loop formed by the thumb.

Step 3: Take the needle back towards the index finger.

Step 4: Take the needle over the top of yarn coming from the index finger to catch it.

Step 5: Next bring the needle back down through the loop on the thumb.

Step 6: Drop loop off the thumb and tighten up the stitch just formed.

You can find a video tutorial here:
youtu.be/etUuAlMVnSk

Two-Colour Long-Tail Cast-On Method

This cast-on is the same as the Long-Tail Cast-On, only with two colours instead of one. Use a colour that contrasts with the main colour, as it will be easier to see where to pick up later.

Begin by knotting the tails of both colours together and then set up as for a Long-Tail Cast-On making sure that the contrast colour is the one going over the thumb. Work as normal for a Long-Tail Cast-On. The main colour should be forming the stitches.

You can find a video tutorial here:
youtu.be/teAlWvapTQA

Reinforcing and Cutting Open Steeks

If you are using a good woolly and grippy yarn like Shetland wool then reinforcing the steek isn't really necessary. However, if you feel more comfortable putting in some reinforcement then I recommend using the Crochet Method.

You will need a crochet hook slightly smaller in size than the needle used for knitting.

For the projects in this book, a 9-stitch vertical striped steek is used. This means that the crochet reinforcement will happen either side of the 5th (centre stitch).

You can find a video tutorial here:
youtu.be/exzYKcSey60

Grafting in Garter Stitch

Make sure needles with live stitches are held parallel. On the front needle, the garter ridge should be sitting close to the needle.

Step 1: Thread a length of working yarn onto a tapestry needle.

Step 2: Bring the needle through the first stitch on the front needle as if to purl and leave on the needle.

Step 3: Bring the needle through the first stitch on the back needle as if to purl and leave on the needle.

Step 4: Bring the needle through the first stitch on the front needle as if to knit and take it off the needle, then go into the next stitch on the same needle as if to purl and leave it on the needle.

Step 5: Bring the needle through the first stitch on the back needle as if to knit and take it off the needle, then bring the needle through the next stitch on the back needle as if to purl and leave it on the needle.

Repeat steps 4+5 until all sts have been grafted making sure to check on your tension as you go.

Wrap and Turn

(RS) Work to the turning point. Slip the next st purlwise to the RH needle and bring the yarn to the front of work between the needles. Slip st back to the LH needle (being careful not to twist stitch). Turn work and bring yarn to the front between the needles, ready to purl the next row. Purl one stitch and then pull on the working yarn to tighten up the wrap.

(WS) Work to the turning point. Slip the next st purlwise to the RH needle and bring the yarn to the back of the work between the needles. Slip st back to the LH needle (being careful not to twist stitch). Turn work and bring yarn to the back between the needles, ready to knit the next row. Knit one stitch and then pull on the working yarn to tighten up the wrap.

Resolving Short Rows
Check that the section of the pattern you are working on requires picking up the wraps. If you do not need to pick up wraps, simply work the wrapped stitches as normal.

(RS) To pick up wraps on the RS, work to wrapped st, insert the right needle from underneath the wrap as if to knit (but do not lift it onto the left needle) and then into the st on the needle and knit together as one.

(WS) To pick up wraps on the WS, work to wrapped st, insert the RH needle from underneath the wrap on the RS of the work and place on left needle and purl it together with the next st on the needle.

Icelandic Cast-Off Method

Begin by knitting 1 stitch, *slip stitch on RH needle to LH needle, insert RH needle into first stitch on LH needle as if to purl and then into the second stitch on LH needle as if to knit, pull that stitch through the first stitch and knit it taking both stitches off the needle; rep from * until 1 stitch remains. Break yarn and draw through remaining stitch.

You can find a video tutorial here: *youtu.be/z82VjfVNRYo*

I-Cord Cast-Off Method

Cast on 3 sts using Backwards-Loop Cast-On, *k2, ssk, slip 3 sts from RH needle back to LH needle; rep from * until you have 3 sts remaining on the LH needle, sk2po, cut yarn leaving tail and draw through remaining st.

Blocking Information

Soak item in a basin of cold or lukewarm water with a gentle wool wash. Make sure that the item is fully soaked and submerged, then leave to soak for at least 20 minutes. If necessary, rinse to remove wool wash. Drain the water away and then gently press down to remove more. Scoop item up carefully and place on towel. Spread the item out a little without pulling excessively and then roll up in the towel to remove more water. Lay the item out on top of a dry towel or blocking mats and block to the measurements desired, paying attention to any areas that need extra emphasis (like the points of the Razor Shell Lace).

Yarn Support

Every design in this book used 100% Shetland wool, as was used in my mother's original knitwear. Jamieson's of Shetland and Jamieson & Smith Shetland Woolbrokers generously contributed the yarn for the samples.

Each design is shown in both companies' versions of 2-ply jumper weight yarn. Most Shetland knitters refer to this weight of yarn as jumper weight. When the first mill spun yarn was produced the weights were named for the item that would be knit using them. Although Jamieson's named their yarn in this weight as Spindrift it is still commonly referred to as jumper weight. Another thing to note is that jumper weight is a 2ply yarn but is the equivalent of 4ply or fingering elsewhere.

Shetland wool has specific qualities that make it especially good for Fair Isle (stranded) knitting. Steek reinforcement is generally not used by Shetland knitters as the wool itself is nice and sticky, so not in danger of unravelling. If substituting for another yarn, try to avoid superwash and look for 100% wool, ideally woollen spun.

If you prefer to use something else, a few substitution suggestions are provided below. Many of the test knitters used these yarns but please don't feel limited to these few suggestions.

- **Tuku Wool Fingering**
- **Harrisville Shetland**
- **Brooklyn Tweed Loft**
- **Holst Garn Supersoft**
- **Elemental Affects Natural Shetland Fingering**
- **Biches & Bûches Le Petit Lambswool**
- **Retrosaria Supersoft**

Abbreviations

approx	Approximately
beg	Beginning
BOR	Beginning of round
CC	Contrast colour
dec(s)	Decrease(s)/Decreasing
est	Established
foll(s)	Follow(s)/Following
G st	Garter stitch
inc(s)	Increase(s)/Increasing
k	Knit
k1-r/b	Knit 1 into row below; Turn the LH needle slightly towards you so that the WS of the work can be seen. Insert RH needle form the top down into the purl stitch that sits below the first st on the LH needle. Knit this stitch then knit the stitch on the needle.
kfb	Knit into the front and back of 1 stitch
k2tog	Knit 2 stitches together
k3tog	Knit 3 stitches together
kwise	Knitwise
LH	Left hand (e.g. LH needle)
MC	Main colour
M1L	Make 1 Left; pick up strand between the two needles from the front to back with the tip of left needle, knit into the back of this stitc
M1R	Make 1 Right; pick up strand between the two needles from back to front with the tip of left needle, knit into the front of this stitch
patt	Pattern (i.e. work in pattern)
PM	Place marker
p	Purl
p2tog	Purl 2 stitches together
prev	Previous
psso	Pass slipped stitch(es) over
p2sso	Pass 2 slipped stitches over
rem(s)	Remain(s)/Remaining
rep	Repeat
RH	Right hand (e.g. RH needle)
RS	Right side of fabric
sl	Slip
ssk	Slip 2 stitches knitwise one at a time, knit together through the back loops
ssk (modified)	Slip first stitch knitwise, slip next stitch purlwise, knit them together through back loop
sssk	Slip 3 stitches knitwise one at a time, knit them together through back loop
SM	Slip marker
sk2po	Sl 1 st knitwise, k2tog, pass slipped stitch over
st(s)	Stitch(es)
St st	Stocking stitch (stockinette): knit on RS rows, purl on WS rows
tbl	Through the back loop
WS	Wrong side of fabric
yo	Yarn over needle and into working position

Acknowledgements

As with any collaborative project, and particularly one that is years in the making, there are many people to thank.

My immense gratitude goes to:

Jen Arnall-Culliford, tech editor extraordinaire. You have no idea how relieved I was when you agreed to take on this project. Thank you for staying on top of the gazillions of emails we must have sent during this process. This book literally would not have come together without you!

My siblings Sorley, Beth, and Jamie. Thank you for your unending love and support, despite our physical distances, and thank you for encouraging me along with this project.

My dad Laughton, for agreeing to write a foreword and for helping me connect the dots and dig up information where possible. Also for all the proud father moments that have buoyed me along the way.

My sister Beth again, for contributing the beautiful leafy watercolours that made this book even more special. Your enthusiasm for all my creative endeavours has meant so much to me.

My daughter Maya, for the gorgeous artwork and rendering in the schematics. Your appreciation of the knitwear and desire to have it all for yourself was also very encouraging!

My husband, David. Your writerly talents helped me make the words in this book infinitely better.

My son, Sage. You have been so complimentary of all the knitwear in this book. I'm sorry none of it fits you, despite your attempts to convince me otherwise. I promise I will include something for you next time!

Tessa Miller, for helping me out last minute and pulling together an epic team for the photoshoot. Your calm and reassurance during this time was just what I needed.

The models Heather and Chelsea, for putting on 100% Shetland wool garments in 90 degree weather in Reno! It was a long day and I greatly appreciate your attitude and patience!

The photographer Ali, for jumping in on this last-minute shoot and doing such a beautiful job of capturing everything.

My dear friend and Shetland adventurer partner Mary Jane Mucklestone, for being by my side when I made discoveries of Mum's knitwear and marvelling at it as much as I did. Your knowledge of Shetland knitting traditions and your talent for Fair Isle design has had a huge influence on me.

Wendy Inkster, for holding onto and treasuring those original jumpers and then so generously gifting them to me. That was a truly special moment.

Wilma Malcolmson, for sharing what you remembered of Mum and always speaking of her so kindly. Thank you also for encouraging me to pursue this revisiting of her work.

Ella Gordon, for helping me get just the right shades for those original sweaters and for cheering enthusiastically at every stage of this project. Your appreciation of vintage knitwear has definitely rubbed off on me!

All the friends and family who bought Mum's pieces in the 70s and held on to them for me to see in person all these years later.

Jamieson's of Shetland and Jamieson & Smith yarn companies for generously donating yarn for the samples.

All the sample knitters, for their impeccable work with each piece. This book would have taken a lot longer if I had been tasked with knitting all the pieces myself!

All the test knitters, for enthusiastically jumping on to make your versions and test out the patterns.

Elizabeth Doherty, for the use of her methodology shaping a sleeve cap with short rows.

Meghan and Lydia of Pom Pom. Thanks for picking up my project and turning it into a reality.

Shetland, for the unending inspiration it provides for knitwear.